Thunderbolt

Thunderbolt

A documentary history of the Republic P-47

Roger Freeman

CHARLES SCRIBNER'S SONS · NEW YORK

First American edition
published by Charles Scribner's Sons, 1979

1 3 5 7 9 11 13 15 17 19   I/C   20 18 16 14 12 10 8 6 4 2

Printed in Great Britain
Library of Congress Catalog Card Number 79-87542
ISBN 0-684-16331-4

Contents

About this Book

The author admits to a long held fascination for the Thunderbolt. As a boy, he worked on the airfield base of the most distinguished of all units, the 56th Group, secretly recording the aircraft decor and watching such famous men as Zemke, Gabreski, Schilling and Robert Johnson in their personal P-47s — at the expense of his agricultural duties! Although admitting to a soft spot for the 56th, his interest frequently drew him to visit the other Thunderbolt airfields. In fact, his notebooks reveal that at one time or another an aircraft of every Eighth and Ninth AF P-47 group passed before his gaze. He also witnessed the toughness of the Thunderbolt in a crash. On one occasion a P-47M was seen to pass between two small oaks which sheared off its wings, the battered fuselage continuing for some 300 yards before coming to a halt. Cut but unbroken, the pilot climbed out and walked away. First-hand experience of the Thunderbolt was the genesis of this book but the greater part of the information and data came from the makers' and Air Force records.

The text embraces a research project on the P-47 carried out in 1970 and further investigations made six years later. There are several areas of the Thunderbolt story where little documentation is available, and others where company and official records conflict. While it is not practical to detail here the exact origin of every fact and figure given in this publication, much of the information was drawn from the following sources: Republic Aviation Corporation (Fairchild) archives; Albert F. Simpson Historical Foundation, Maxwell AFB; National Archives and Smithsonian Museum, Washington; Air Force Museum, Dayton; 1361st Photo Squadron, USAF, Arlington; Pratt & Whitney Aircraft; Hamilton Standard; Curtiss Aviation; Imperial War Museum, London; Public Record Office, London; and RAF Museum, Hendon.

Additional documents, information and assistance came from the following individuals: Serge Blandin, N. E. Borden, Norman Brown, Mike Bailey, Art Beltrone, Allan Blue, Ron Capewell, Frank Cheesman, Urban Drew, Jim Double, Virginia Finsic, Royal Frey, Garry Fry, Cass Hough, Robert Jones, A. J. Knight, Robert Keeler, Witold Lanowski, Harvey Lippincott, David Menard, Ian Mactaggart, George Pennick, Robert Mikesh, Kenn Rust, Harold G. Martin, Bruce Riglesford, Jim Wogsted and Gerrie Zwanenburg.

The drawings of the P-47 were made by Norman Ottaway, consuming some eighty hours of his time over many months. He insisted on starting 'from scratch' and with the aid of Dave Menard's and Jim Wogsted's measurements taken from captive museum Thunderbolts, produced a set of plans which are really new and not based on other published drawings. As both draughtsman and enthusiast, Norman demands meticulous accuracy and honesty. Indeed, even a deficiency of one half-inch in the undercarriage track was not to be overlooked!

Special mention should also be made of Dave Menard, who gallantly undertook many an exacting stint at a microfilm viewer in order to track down the serial numbers of P-47s going to foreign powers.

On the production side I wish to acknowledge Charles W. Cain's guidance with the original project, Jean Freeman's perserverence at the typewriter, John W. Archer's eagle-eye in proof reading and Bruce Robertson for his most helpful editorial advice.

In addition to the large number of USAAF and maker's documents consulted, a bibliography of published work perused included *Combat Squadrons of the Air Force, World War II* edited by Maurer Maurer, *Fighter Squadrons of the RAF* by John Rawlings, *The 56th Fighter Group in World War II*, *The Army Air Forces in World War II, Vols I-V*, Craven & Cate, and magazine articles *POA Fighter Markings* by Kenn C. Rust in the AAHS Journal, and *Whine From The Jug* by Warren Bodie in Wings/Airpower.

Roger A. Freeman
1978

Introduction

The Republic P-47 Thunderbolt was truly a redoubtable fighter aircraft of World War 2. Some of its contemporaries may have become more famous through the particular nature of their involvement in that conflict, but the Thunderbolt was as worthy as any. Few pilots detailed to fly the Thunderbolt in battle over a period of time failed to appreciate its dependability, durability and devastating firepower; qualities which made it without par for ground-attack sorties. No other single-seat fighter of World War 2 afforded a pilot a better chance of survival. Although the largest and heaviest single piston-engined fighter ever flown in World War 2 combat, this did surprisingly little to detract from its value as an air fighting vehicle. In fact, the majority of the top American fighter aces engaged with the German Luftwaffe used the Thunderbolt. Understood and skilfully piloted, the Thunderbolt could be made to hold its own with the best of adversaries. Large in size, it was also built in larger quantities than any other United States fighter aircraft. The Republic Thunderbolt was, in some measure, a reflection of the character of the nation from whence it sprang: generous in proportions, with any shortcomings totally eclipsed by undeniable superlatives.

Roger A. Freeman

1 From Russia with Ambition

In the Bolshevik revolution of 1917 may be found the root cause of many happenings that shaped the subsequent history of the 20th Century. An outcome of this violent time was that many Russians, neither safe nor welcome in their homeland, were obliged to seek a new life in other countries where more tolerant political regimes prevailed.

One such emigrant was Alexander P. Seversky – a native of Tiflis, Georgia – whose father had been the first private-owner pilot in Imperial Russia. In 1914 young Seversky learned to fly on a Farman biplane while training at the Russian Military School of Aeronautics. Commissioned as a Sub-Lieutenant in the Imperial Naval Air Service, he was posted to a seaplane bomber squadron based on Oesel (Saaremaa) Island in the Baltic Sea. On a night operation on July 1915, his aircraft was shot down and exploded on crashing. Seversky, escaping with his life, lost his right leg. After convalescing, during which he helped supervise seaplane construction, he received special permission from the Tsar to return to combat flying. Promoted to Lieutenant Commander, Seversky first commanded a bombing squadron and then created a reputation as a successful fighter pilot, destroying 13 German aircraft in combat and being awarded some of Imperial Russia's highest decorations.

In September 1917, Seversky was sent via France to the United States of America as vice-chairman of a Naval Air Mission. Following the October Revolution he decided to remain in the USA and worked for the Army Air Service as a consultant engineer, more specifically as a special assistant to Brigadier-General William 'Billy' Mitchell. In 1922, the US Government purchased the rights of 364 aeronautical patents, including a bombsight that Seversky had registered, for $50,000. With the sum, he formed his first company – the Seversky Aero Corporation.

Alexander Kartveli was another Russian on a mission to the West who did not return. Also born in Tiflis, birthplace of Iosif Stalin (Dzhugashvili), he was a military cadet at St Petersburg Academy when World War 1 broke out. He was sent as an artillery officer to the Turkish front where later he was wounded in action.

By early 1918 Imperial Russia was in chaos and Georgia began setting up its own administration. A few selected officers, Kartveli among them, were sent to Paris to study French military tactics. Soon all the Russias were engulfed by revolution and counter-revolution. Kartveli, like Seversky, was left without a country. He became a circus trapeze artist and taught mathematics to gain the means to attain his ambition – degrees in aeronautical and electrical engineering. There followed design and development periods with French companies including Blériot-Aeronautique, Avions Michel Wibault, Avions Bernard Ferbois and the Société de Télémécanique, but none of these positions gave Kartveli real satisfaction and he considered advancing his career elsewhere.

At the beginning of July 1927 Kartveli's opportunity came in a meeting with Charles A. Levine, President of the embryo Columbia Aircraft Corporation of New York. Through dealings in scrap, Levine had become a dollar millionaire at 30 and was busy spending part of his fortune on his current passion for flying. An ambition was to secure the $25,000 Raymond Orteig prize for the first non-stop New York–Paris flight, but while he was preparing Charles Lindbergh made his historic flight. However, Levine decided to continue with his plans and some two weeks after Lindbergh, on 4 June, he set out over the Atlantic in his Bellanca WB-2 monoplane *Miss Columbia* piloted by Clarence D. Chamberlain. After 43 hours in the air, they landed about 100 miles south-west of Berlin and Levine could claim to be the first trans-Atlantic aircraft passenger. Both men were given heroes' welcomes in Berlin and other European capitals before they eventually arrived in Paris on 30 June.

At the fateful meeting in Paris, it is related that neither Levine nor Kartveli could speak the other's language, but Kartveli's design studies must have impressed the shrewd but mercurial millionaire. Levine immediately invited Kartveli to come to the United

States and work for him at Columbia Aircraft Corporation. This association with Levine's enterprise was not particularly successful and the aircraft Kartveli designed was destroyed in a hangar fire. After leaving, his abilities and qualifications earned him a post with Fokker (Atlantic Aircraft Corporation) at their New Jersey plant.

Meanwhile, the dashing Major de Seversky (US Army Reserve rank; the 'de' style adopted while in France) had not enjoyed any great success with his original enterprise. So, in February 1931, he formed a new company, Seversky Aircraft Corporation, and obtained sufficient financial backing to engage in limited aircraft design and construction. Not only was Seversky founder and president of the new company, but also chief designer and test pilot. Having met Kartveli and established a friendship through a common bond of language and origin, it was natural that Seversky should invite Kartveli to join him in the venture. Kartveli began as assistant chief engineer but soon assumed prime responsibility for all designs.

The initial Seversky design constructed at his Farmingdale, Long Island, plant was an exciting looking, three-seat, radial-engine floatplane which, it was hoped, would appeal to both civil and military markets. Known as the SEV-3 – an abbreviation of Seversky three-place – it was to appear in a number of guises as its creators sought to gain orders for their business. First flown by Seversky in June 1933, the SEV-3 went on to give many demonstration flights before being returned to the factory to re-appear with floats replaced by a trousered main undercarriage and a big spatted tailwheel. Next it became an amphibian and on 15 September 1935 at Detroit, Seversky established a world speed record for amphibians, averaging slightly over 230 mph. However, the civil market could not give the company sufficient orders to consolidate the SEV-3 as a viable manufacturing proposition.

In common with most manufacturers at that time, Seversky kept a watchful eye on the military scene. The limited orders US Army Air Corps or US Navy funds allowed were very much a lifeline in the 'make-or-break' existence confronting small aircraft companies in the United States.

The Army Air Corps Materiel Division practice was to issue design competitions for aircraft to meet specific requirements, and it was up to interested manufacturers to submit a tender and prototype by given dates. Thus, in 1935, when the Air Corps announced a requirement for a monoplane-type standard basic trainer, Seversky Aircraft Corporation adapted their pioneer SEV-3 design to accord with the Army's specification. For Seversky, winning this competition and being awarded an initial contract for 30 BT-8 aircraft (USAAC Basic Trainer Type Eight) was an historic event.

The previous year the company had set about building a second design, a two-seat monoplane much along the same lines, designated SEV-2XP (Seversky Two-place Experimental Pursuit). This was evolved to meet an Air Corps requirement for a pursuit competition scheduled for June 1935. Unfortunately while being flown from Farmingdale to Wright Field, Dayton, Ohio, for evaluation, the SEV-2XP was damaged in an accident and, in its original configuration (and designation) was never officially tested.

During repair the opportunity was taken to advance the design by installing a rearwards retracting main undercarriage and to rework the cockpit for single-seat operation. Suitably modified, the prototype re-emerged from the Farmingdale workshops as SEV-1XP in time to compete in the postponed pursuit competition at Wright Field in August 1935. Further modifications were effected prior to evaluation, notably the installation of a new engine. The Air Corps found the Seversky SEV-1XP agile and pleasant to fly. They were particularly impressed by its endurance permitting a range in excess of 1,000 miles at 250 mph. However, top speed fell short of the manufacturers objective of 300 mph, the best figure obtained being 289 mph, and the underpowered 850 hp Wright Cyclone radial engine gave other problems. Even so, the Air Corps engineers preferred the aircraft to that of its competition rival, the Curtiss 75. Once more there were delays – this time because of Curtiss's valid complaint that Seversky had been unfairly allowed extra time to enhance their entry. By April 1936 when the pursuit competition was re-opened two other contenders, Consolidated and Vought, joined the Curtiss and Seversky at Wright Field.

In the intervening months Kartveli had substituted an 850 hp Pratt & Whitney Twin Wasp radial for the Cyclone, fitted revised shape tail surfaces and incorporated other refinements which carried the Air Corps' decision in the SEV-1XP's favour. An order for 77, worth $1,636,250, to be designated P-35 (Pursuit type 35), came from the War Department in 1936 and delivery took place between July 1937 and August 1938.

Probably the most outstanding feature of the P-35 was its range of 1,150 miles; some 400 miles better than any of the competing designs and three times as great as the Boeing P-26 and other Air Corps' pursuit

Right Seversky's first export order – 1935 – was for three SEV-3M-WW reconnaissance amphibians for the Colombian Air Force. Quasi-elliptical wing shape would be perpetuated through other designs. *Below* Alexander Kartveli, aircraft designer extraordinary. Born on 9 September 1896 he died on 20 July 1974; this picture was taken in his seventieth year. (Republic).

Middle right The original Seversky, with a spatted undercarriage replacing the amphibian twin-float arrangement, photographed over New York in May 1934 with the Major piloting. (Charles W. Cain Collection)

Right The Seversky 2PA-A (Two-place, Pursuit Aircraft, Amphibian) was built to a Soviet order and delivered to the USSR in the spring of 1938.

Left SEV-1XP against the favourite background for Seversky air photography. (Republic) *Below* The British Experimental Demonstrator, 2PA-BX at Martlesham Heath in March 1939. (British Official) *Bottom* AP-1 was a Seversky P-35 development aircraft, here seen fitted with a large spinner, the object being to improve performance through better streamlining.

aircraft then in squadron service. Good range potential was advocated by Seversky and became an inherent feature of the later designs which, following the financial boost from the P-35 order, came with imaginative profusion as the company sought new outlets for business. Its first sales had been a few amphibians to Colombia and in 1937 a successful transaction with Japan resulted in 20 Seversky 2PA-L two-seat fighters being delivered in 1938. Intended for bomber escort the Japanese found this 'convoy fighter' heavier and less manoeuvrable than expected and eventually employed the 2PA-L on reconnaissance duties over the Chinese battle fronts. In the same year an export order was obtained from the Soviet Union for two examples of similar two-place fighters, one an amphibian, an order that must have given the two emigrée Alexanders from Georgia a special satisfaction.

The Company was not slow in appreciating the potential market for military aircraft in Europe, where a civil war raged in Spain and a resurgent Germany had a massive rearmament programme in progress. But, spurred by the fear of war, the development of fighter aircraft had proceeded apace with the major powers, Britain, France, Germany and Italy, so that the Seversky monoplane was generally inferior in both performance and equipment to its European contemporaries. Only Sweden showed real interest in the export variant of the P-35 demonstrated to them in 1938, and they were similarly approving of a two-seat version that followed.

In the civil field, Seversky gained considerable prestige from the many speed records obtained with non-military variants of the developed landplane design. In September 1937, the Bendix Air Race, a premier event in the United States aviation calendar, was won by Frank W. Fuller in a Seversky averaging 258 mph from Burbank, California, to Cleveland, Ohio. The same year, Jacqueline Cochran broke the women's international three-kilometre record during the Detroit National Air Show in a similar Seversky averaging 293 mph. On one lap Miss Cochran reached 304.7 mph, a sensational figure at a time when many Air Corps and Navy pursuit aircraft had top speeds of around 200 mph. She went on to win the 1938 Bendix in a Seversky, and the following year another P-35 derivative took first place for the third year in succession. These and similar achievements did much to advertise the combination of high cruise speed and range inherent in Seversky monoplanes.

All these aircraft, export and racing models, were based on the same primary design and powered either by Wright or Pratt & Whitney radial engines. This exploitation of the basic airframe made good business sense in a small aircraft manufacturing concern by making maximum use of special construction jigs, obtaining better return from labour through increasing familiarity with components which brought enhanced expertise and smoother production. Even so, and despite the Company's successes in obtaining further orders from the Air Corps and abroad, the huge cost of running such an enterprise began to tell.

By 1939 a financial crisis loomed and could only be settled by new capital. The money was found but the investors were naturally entitled to reorganise the company as they saw fit. This culminated in Major de Seversky relinquishing his presidency and William Kellett (a former vice-president or director) being appointed in his place. Ironically, from then on the Company never looked back, as in the same month Sweden placed the largest order so far received for Seversky aircraft: 120 P-35 fighters.

The design team remained much the same with Kartveli continuing as chief engineer, still pursuing the policy of advancing his basic airframe. With the troubled world scene, even the isolationist United States was moved to strengthen its armed forces, and more funds were made available for equipment.

The success of the P-35 was short-lived, for the Air Corps soon ordered a Curtiss fighter (P-36) based on the earlier Curtiss 75, which had a better performance than the P-35 in most respects except manoeuvrability and range. Speed was of prime consideration for pursuits and Kartveli sought means of obtaining 300 mph from his basic design. Airframe manufacturers, constantly demanding more power for their designs, accelerated the development of aero-engines. By 1938 Pratt & Whitney had an upgraded version of their Twin Wasp radial capable of producing 1,150 hp and available with an integral supercharger to help maintain power in the rarified air at altitude. Increased power was only one factor for faster speeds; another was a cleaner airframe, achieved by the replacement of the almost totally exposed rearwards-retracting main undercarriage by a completely flush-fitting inwards-retracting assembly. Both these improvements were proposed to the Air Corps who scheduled the last production P-35 airframe to incorporate these features, giving this prototype a new type designation, XP-41.

The XP-41 was completed early in 1939 and was later tested at Wright Field. It could attain more than 320 mph at 15,000 ft and retain the P-35's advantages in manoeuvrability and range. However, the Air Corps considered that the advance over its forbear was insufficient to warrant production. They were, in any case, more interested in an alternative private venture development by the Company which had a turbo-supercharger to boost altitude performance still further. As altitude increases the air density decreases and offers less resistance to an airframe being propelled through it, with consequent opportunities for higher speeds. Against this advantage, the thinner air provides insufficient oxygen for a maximum-power combustible mixture to be fed by the carburettors to the engines. In other words, the higher an aero-engine is taken, the less oxygen there is available and the greater the fall-off in power. Hence the application of superchargers, which compress air to a density equal to sea-level conditions and feeds it to the engine to enable low altitude power to be obtained at high altitude. The geared supercharger fitted to the XP-41's engine had its limitations, whereas the turbo-supercharger – which used engine exhaust gases to work the air compressor – offered much better possibilities for improved performance.

Kartveli's team appreciated that it was in the upper atmosphere that they could best seek to enhance the speed and agility of their basic airframe. The turbo-supercharger was both bulky and heavy and its accommodation in the airframe was not easily accomplished. It was installed in the fuselage at a point near the centre of gravity, with ducting to and from the engine and a waist gate to expel the used exhaust gases under the fuselage amidships. This aircraft, known by the company designation AP-4 (Army Pursuit No.4), was delivered to Wright Field for comparative trials early in 1939. Top speeds in the region of 350 mph were obtained at 20,000 ft and although performance fell away at further altitude, the AP-4 could reach 38,000 ft. In March 1939 an order for 13 service test models – under the designation YP-43 (Y prefix indicating test) – was forthcoming from the Air Corps who, with a number of other promising fighter designs in view, would not be committed to large-scale production orders at this juncture. Later in the year a yet more powerful development of AP-4 with cleaned-up airframe was proposed. On the strength of preliminary design work a straight off-the-drawing-board production run of 80 such aircraft was ordered in September under the designation P-44. Governmental fears that the nation might soon be embroiled in war caused the Air Corps to dispense with the prototype stage to hasten introduction, the P-44 being based on a well-proven design and being basically an up-rated YP-43.

Other American manufacturers were turning from radial engines to the new Allison liquid-cooled in-line engine to power their fighter designs because the combination of high power output and small frontal area offered better streamlining prospects. But early high powered in-line engines had extremely large water-cooled radiators that were an obstacle to good aerodynamics until the coolant Glycol became available in the 1930s. This had good heat dispersing properties permitting smaller radiator area. At this time both the Air Corps and American aircraft industry were beginning to wake up to the advances in fighter development in Europe, where designs such as the Hurricane, Spitfire, Dewoitine D 520 and the Messerschmitt Bf 109 all employed liquid-cooled motors. Nevertheless, it is noteworthy that the evaluation officers at Wright Field refused to put all the (pursuit) eggs in one basket, perhaps as the result of some personal experience with the troublesome early liquid-cooled engines against the comparatively reliable radials.

Seversky Aircraft Corporation, however, could not ignore the potential of the new Allison 'Vee' – a popular term for liquid-cooled engines where cylinders were arranged in two banks, V-positioned to the crank case when viewed head-on. During the summer of 1939, Kartveli worked on a completely new design proposal featuring the Allison as a powerplant and with an airframe of similar weights and characteristics to European trends in interceptors. This proposal for Seversky model AP-10 was submitted for evaluation in August 1939, a few weeks prior to Hitler's invasion of Poland leading to Britain and France becoming involved in the conflict known as the Second World War.

The Army Board convened to evaluate AP-10 recommended that, while they did not consider it suitable for production, it possessed sufficient desirable characteristics to warrant further investigation as an experimental aeroplane. Basically, Kartveli had set out to design an extremely light-weight interceptor, with about the smallest airframe that could be built around the Allison. The Experimental Engineering section of Wright Field then went to work on the design and made detail changes involving raising the weight from 4,600 to 4,900 lb and increasing the wing area from 110 to 115 sq ft. Provision was also made for bomb racks under the wings. Armament remained as originally proposed by Seversky, fuselage-mounted 0.50-in and 0.30-in machine-guns. Top speed was to be 415 mph obtained at 15,000 ft and it had to reach this height from take-off in $3\frac{1}{2}$ minutes.

A contract, prepared in early November, provided

Right The first YP-43, highly polished for evaluation trials. Viewed from this angle it bears a striking resemblance to the Thunderbolt. *Below* A P-35 of the 31st Pursuit Group, which was based at Selfridge Field, Michigan in 1940. (Fred C. Dickey)

Right Republic Lancers of the 1st Pursuit Group, decked out with green crosses for the 1941 'war games'. First air-cooled engined fighter with a turbo-supercharger to equip Air Corps squadrons, it was quickly relegated to second-line duties when the US became involved in hostilities. (Walter Knight)

Left A Chinese Air Force P-43A-1 with D/F aerial under the fuselage. An extra 205 Lancers were manufactured at Farmingdale during 1941 to keep the plant fully active.

Above The XP-47B May 1941. Although the aircraft handled well on its first flight, the cockpit filled with smoke and Lowery Brabham terminated the trip at Mitchel Field earlier than planned. Here the cause of the smoke was found to be oil that had accumulated in ducting and been heated by the exhaust.

Left The XP-47B: June 1942. On 8 August it was destroyed when Republic test pilot Fillmore Gilmer abandoned the aircraft over Long Island Sound when the rear fuselage caught fire. Gilmer's parachute descent was observed and he was quickly retrieved from the water by the crew of a launch.

for two prototypes designated XP-47 and XP-47A. The XP-47A was to be identical with XP-47 except that it was to be delivered first, within nine months, and would be devoid of armament, radio and other tactical equipment so that flight testing could be accomplished ahead of the fully combat-equipped XP-47. The contract was not approved, for the authorising agency in Washington, DC, considered the XP-47 had insufficient firepower; also, it possessed too high a wing loading and too low a top speed in comparison with the contemporary Curtiss XP-46 fighter. As a result of the contract rejection discussions between designers and Air Corps engineers led to a still larger aircraft with wing area expanded to 165 sq ft. Firepower was increased to a pair of 0.30-in machine-guns in each wing, and two 0.50s in the fuselage synchronised to fire through the propeller arc. The design weight was advanced to 6,150 lb but a top speed of 400 mph at 15,000 ft was still expected although the time to that altitude was extended to $4\frac{3}{4}$ minutes. A new contract was prepared and approved in January 1940.

By then, the United States aircraft industry was expanding not only on the strength of orders placed by a wary government but through large orders from other powers, notably Britain and France. While the European air experts who came to evaluate the designs were admirers of the sound construction and good flying qualities of most American aircraft, they were critical of their value in combat. These sentiments were echoed by official US military observers visiting the war fronts in western Europe, albeit the storm had yet to break. By the early months of 1940 the message had begun to have some effect upon Air Corps leaders, that their aircraft were generally deficient in firepower, protective armour for aircrew and vulnerable components, and lacking such technical advances as self-sealing fuel tanks. Nowhere were these weaknesses so marked as in the pursuits available. The standard Air Corps pursuit aircraft of the late 1930s was seen as an old-fashioned, two-gun cowboy, whereas the British equivalent was a steel-helmeted, battle-dressed soldier armed with automatic weapons.

Within a month of approving the contract for the XP-47, the Air Corps Materiel Division wrote to the manufacturers – who had changed their company name to Republic Aviation Corporation in October 1939 – requesting their estimate of the effect of incorporating self-sealing tanks, pilot armour and other war equipment. On 27 February 1940 Republic replied that this equipment would entail adding an extra 5 sq ft of wing area to maintain the specified wing loading since the gross weight of the aircraft would

increase by 200 lb. Climbing time and take-off and landing runs would be affected and provision for carrying underwing bombs would have to be eliminated. Further, most of the engineering work already undertaken would have to be scrapped, delivery of the prototype would take an extra 45 days and the cost of the changes was estimated at $15,000. Further correspondence and discussion ensued and once more the plan for XP-47 was revamped. Total weight increase would be 250 lb and the prototype would be delayed 60 days.

Concerned at the shortcomings in its pursuit aircraft highlighted by developments in Europe, the Air Corps convened a special Board to consider the whole question of fighter design and procurement. By May 1940, it was apparent that its members were not satisfied with the XP-47 which seemed likely to have difficulty in meeting a specification that was already near to being outdated. The Board also considered that too great a proportion of the current pursuit aircraft programme was dependent upon the satisfactory development of the Allison engine and that work on interceptors making use of air-cooled or other types of liquid-cooled engines should be expedited to the full.

Anticipating the death knell for XP-47, Republic turned their attention to the use of Pratt & Whitney's new radial, the XR-2800 Double Wasp, offering 2,000 hp. This large engine, already considered as a power plant for the advanced P-44 version of the Company's basic radial-engine fighter airframe, presented many design problems; indeed the airframe that had evolved from old SEV-1XP had just about reached the limit of its development as a pursuit vehicle. As the XP-47 was far too small to take the Double Wasp, it was obvious that Kartveli must design a completely new airframe if this powerful engine was to be employed and all the special paraphernalia of war incorporated without difficulty. On 12 June 1940, a date which saw a triumphant German army fanning out along the French coast, Republic Aviation submitted a revised specification for their XP-47 contract, which substituted a Pratt & Whitney R-2800 radial for the Allison V-1710 originally planned. The characteristics given for this new XP-47B model, were a top speed of 400 mph at 25,000 ft, reducing to 340 mph at 5,000 ft; a time to 15,000 ft of five minutes. The armament of six 0.50-in machine-guns brought the design gross weight up to 11,600 lb. This was a startling specification, considering that the weight was more than twice that originally projected for XP-47. Nevertheless, the high-altitude performance – and the proposed armament – was better than

Above Early Thunderbolts being flown by Republic test pilots, late June 1942. Nearest camera is the third line-production P-47B which has an experimental flat panel cockpit windshield and sliding canopy installed on a fuselage laid down for the hinged type of XP-47B. Pilot is Lowery Brabham who made the first flight in a Thunderbolt. Second aircraft, 41-5930, is a then new P-47B with standardised cockpit glazing. Third aircraft in the flight is the XP-47B which retains its original hinged hood. *Left* The Man and the Machine: Kartveli poses in front of a Thunderbolt. (Republic) *Right* P-47C introduced metal covered rudder and elevators into production plus other refinements although first examples were otherwise similar to late B models. (Republic)

Right Out to grass. A few P-47Bs survived to the end of hostilities. Awaiting dispersal, the yellow cowl and tail on 41-5983 attest to its use in a training role. (Harold Martin) *Below* Pratt & Whitney engineers run up a P-47B used for test purposes. This aircraft was re-worked and has the modified fin and all-metal covered rudder and elevators. (Pratt & Whitney)

any other pursuit project currently under development for the Air corps. US observers had been impressed by the British eight-gun fighters but the weapons now proposed for XP-47B were not the 0.303-in rifle-calibre types of the Spitfire and Hurricane but the US Army's heavy-calibre machine-gun; although the rate of fire was about two-thirds that of the smaller weapon and the weight three times as much, the charge and bullets were larger, giving superior muzzle velocity, range and penetration. Impressed with this high altitude interceptor, large and heavy as it was, the Air Corps approved the change, although not officially until 6 September 1940. In the meantime work on the XP-47 and XP-47A was terminated, and practically all engineering development plus the construction of certain detail parts were scrapped, in all costing some $60,000. A full-scale wind tunnel model of the XP-47 was in an advanced state of construction when plans were changed and it was decided to complete this and turn it over to the National Advisory Committee on Aeronautics (NACA) at Langley Field, Virginia, for use in investigating the general cooling requirements of the Allison engine.

The design problems facing Kartveli's team in that fateful summer of 1940 were nothing less than formidable. The aircraft they planned to build was unique in many respects and called for much ingenuity although the engineering experience gained over the many years with the Seversky monoplane pursuit stood them in good stead. Visually, the XP-47B as projected by Kartveli was a 'stretched' version of its radial forerunners. The elliptical wings and deep fuselage that characterised those designs were retained, but the elongation gave the XP-47B a more refined and less dumpy appearance. Structurally, many of the proven methods employed on the early designs were repeated but for the most part the problems involved required new procedures. To surpass 400 mph at high altitude, a perfect ducting link with the huge turbo-supercharger was essential. As with the YP-43 the turbo-supercharger was placed in the fuselage aft of the pilot. To ensure the most efficient and least interrupted air flow to this unit, the ducting was designed first and then the fuselage built-up around it. This ducting for exhaust gases and air was arranged along the bottom of the fuselage and would come to have another important property, not envisaged by its designers.

To take full advantage of the power available and the gearing of the engine, a 4-blade controllable-pitch propeller was specified, the first for a modern US military aircraft. This brought another problem as the

12 ft 2 in diameter of the propeller necessitated unusually long main undercarriage legs to obtain sufficient ground clearance. In turn, suspension points were required so far outboard on the wing that it would be impossible to install the three or four wing guns specified. A solution was eventually found in a telescoping landing gear that would be 9 in longer when extended than when retracted and stowed in the wing. This arrangement allowed efficient wing structure and left room for the full eight-gun armament if required. The thirsty engine would require generous fuel tankage and furthering the company's reputation for aircraft with good endurance, two internal tanks were installed forward and below the cockpit with a combined holding of approximately 300 US gallons.

To bring the P-47 series into production required many months of preparation and expansion of the factory to meet the $56,499,923 order for 773 aircraft placed in September 1940. The fighter was, in fact, being ordered off-the-drawing-board before the prototype had flown and proved its worth. Acceptance of the P-47 design had also brought the abandonment of the P-44, which had foundered on the Air Corps' requirements for armour protection and increased firepower, imposing unacceptable weight and stress factors on the airframe. To keep the existing production lines active, further versions of the YP-43 type were ordered under the designations P-43 and P-43A. Even before they appeared they were considered second-line aircraft to be relegated to operational training and other duties.

The P-43 came to be known as the Lancer. The British policy of giving names to aircraft had caught on in the USA, largely through those bestowed on US-manufactured aircraft for the RAF. C.Hart Miller, Republic's Director of Military Contracts, thought up Thunderbolt for the XP-47B and the Company approved this name. By 6 May 1941, when test pilot Lowery L. Brabham flew the XP-47B from the Farmingdale runway on its initial flight, the name Thunderbolt was already well known. A 'Thunderbolt March' was composed and a great deal of flag-waving ballyhoo attended the aircraft's debut. Across the Atlantic British newspapers and journals politely repeated the claims of 'fastest and best' without comment. The RAF, no doubt cautioned by its experience of American fighters so far received, remained slightly sceptical. From Germany came words of derision. The largest, heaviest, single-seat fighter the world had seen, sat in a hanger at Farmingdale. The question now was would it come to justify the implications of its name?

2 Trouble and Troubleshooters

The first production Thunderbolt was really a specially built second prototype and on completion in December 1941 was despatched to Wright Field. This P-47B, serial 41-5895, was used as Army Air Forces' test aircraft (the Air Corps became the Air Forces in June 1941) while XP-47B remained with the manufacturer. The first four P-47Bs from production appeared in mid-March 1942 and were to be used for an extensive test programme by various agencies. Last of these, 41-5899, on an early flight, crashed on Salisbury golf course, Long Island, on 26 March killing Republic test pilot George Burrell. The P-47B was totally destroyed but examination of the wreckage revealed that part of the tail assembly had broken away in flight. This tragedy brought restriction of P-47 flying while the cause of the structural failure was investigated. Fabric on the elevators was found ruptured, high speed flight pressures having caused it to balloon with disastrous effects on control. Eventually a solution was found with metal covered elevators. However, the problem was not solved without further loss. On 1 May Republic pilot Joe Parker was test-flying the sixth P-47B, 41-5900, over Oak Beach, New York, when he lost all elevator control. Happily Parker survived, being the first man to successfully parachute from a Thunderbolt, although he ended up in the water off Long Island Sound. Some time elapsed before metal tail control surfaces could be incorporated in production and in the meantime Thunderbolts were delivered with the intention that modifications would be effected later. The acceptance of P-47B 41-5904 on 26 May marked the start of a flow of Thunderbolts to the Army Air Forces (AAF) that would soon reach a rate of 50 per month.

Shortly after the Japanese attack on Pearl Harbor and the United States' involvement in war with the Axis powers, steps were taken to bolster the air defences around New York. The ingenuity of the Germans was such that it was not inconceivable, although highly unlikely in view of the distances involved, that some form of aerial attack could be mounted. Thus, in January 1942, came a decision to move a partly-trained fighter group of three squadrons to the New England coast area, starting a chain of events that would come to have a special place in the history of aerial warfare.

The 56th Pursuit Group had been created a year before in sunny Carolina. Now it was to take its motley collection of Bell P-39 Airacobras and other fighter aircraft to the wintery north-east, settling one squadron at Bridgeport in Connecticut, another at Bendix, New Jersey, and the third on a newly prepared site at Farmingdale, Long Island, not far from Republic Aviation Corporation's plant. The Company was about to turn out the first production models of the Thunderbolt, its large radial-engine fighter, with performance details still officially secret but a good talking point for men of the 56th. The Thunderbolt was rumoured to weigh six tons, a factor which just did not make sense to the pursuit pilots. While the P-39s of the 56th flew patrols along the New England seaboard, or were hurriedly 'scrambled' to meet unidentified aircraft, other decisions were being made by higher authority. Full-scale testing and assessment of operational problems could only be achieved quickly by putting the aircraft into the hands of a fully-fledged service unit. The 56th Group, being in part on Republic's doorstep, was selected to be first to fly the mighty Thunderbolt. Another, new, fighter group, the 80th, was also moved into Farmingdale with the intention that it too would start training on P-47s.

The P-47B, although incorporating many internal refinements in the light of experience with the XP-47B prototype, was outwardly identical, apart from a sliding cockpit hood and repositioned aerial mast. The hinged hood on XP-47B was awkward and in an emergency could hinder a hasty exit from the cockpit. Performance was much in line with Kartveli's proposal two years previously. Even so, the aircraft was some 650 lb heavier than planned and, in consequence, climb to 15,000 ft took 6.7 minutes as against a predicted five. However, the top speed was nearly 30 mph faster at 429 mph.

The second P-47B and other early examples went to

Right A formation of 56th FG P-47Bs over the Atlantic seaboard on a fine October day, 1942. Leading aircraft is the Group Commander's 'ship' piloted by Colonel Hubert Zemke, and wearing the red, yellow and blue colours of the three component squadrons in fusclage bands and tri-sected cowling ring. Other Thunderbolts have red noses and are assigned to 61st FS. *Left and Below* Cockpit instrumentation and controls in P-47B 41-6038 and P-47D-2-RE, 42-8009. Power control quadrant is on the left side with electrical switching below. Both these particular aircraft were used for experimental work. The P-47B served as an engine test bed for Ford at Ypailanti, Detroit where R-2800-59s were built, while the P-47D was used to test dive flaps. A special tachometer in connection with the latter can be seen attached to the upper left side of the instrument shroud.

REPUBLIC P-47 THUNDERBOLT

the Republic Mechanics School, providing the ground crews of the 56th and 80th with a foretaste of the engineering and maintenance task. The radial engine was easily accessible by the removal of quick-release cowling sections, and offered fewer maintenance tasks than the liquid-cooled Allisons that had been the ground crews' preoccupation with the P-39. The most complex area of the aircraft was the mass of hydraulic lines and electrical cables linking various components with the many controls and instruments in the cockpit. It was this array of levers and dials, confronting anyone climbing into the cockpit, that tended to unnerve the novice pilot. The situation was not quite as bad as it looked when it came to flying the aircraft, for most of the instrumentation and switches were connected with refinements that gave the pilot precise control over many factors influencing the performance of the fighter. There was nothing 'utility' about the P-47 – its designers had gone all the way in providing the best they could to ensure a first-class flying and fighting vehicle.

By mid-June 1942, sufficient Thunderbolts were available for flight training to begin in earnest. Because it grossed some six short tons the P-47B required a take-off run of nearly half-a-mile to become airborne over a 50 ft high obstacle. To give newcomers an ample safety margin most first flights were from Mitchel Field, New York, or Bradley Field at Windsor Locks, Connecticut, where the runaways were over a mile long. Bridgeport Municipal Airport, where the headquarters and two squadrons of the 56th were then housed, was not so generously endowed and once a take-off run was well under way a pilot was totally committed to getting the Thunderbolt airborne. Failure often meant a crash into the sea. The teething troubles which showed up during these early and, of necessity, cautious flights were chiefly with hydraulic and electrical items – flaws in production that were not too difficult to solve. But so much was new about the Thunderbolt – aero-engine, propeller, and numerous minor components – that some malfunctioning was almost inevitable. Added to this were the difficulties experienced by pilots in mastering the ways of a fighter quite unlike anything they had previously flown. Accidents became a worrying feature of the P-47's service introduction and by the end of June the 56th Group had damaged or wrecked half those received.

The reactions of pilots during transition to the P-47 followed a pattern. At first, the sheer size and apparent sophistication of the aircraft instilled extreme caution. With the confidence of increasing familiarity came the desire to discover just how fast and furiously the air-craft would travel through the upper air. For it was at altitudes above 20,000 ft that the Thunderbolt really began to impress. Whereas a pilot was conscious that he was in charge of a big aeroplane in the denser atmosphere, at five miles above the earth the P-47 was quite different. It was more nimble and given to pushing the pointer of the air speed indicator towards the 400 mph mark at the slightest provocation.

In a dive especially, the speed of the P-47B built up alarmingly and it was not long before a pilot in his P-47 – last heard of from at 30,000 ft – was discovered at the bottom of a deep crater in a farmer's field. Similar fatalities followed and it was evident that at high speeds loss of control was occurring. Evidence soon turned up in the form of a mangled rudder ripped from a P-47B in flight. Torn, buckled and distorted rudders on other Thunderbolts that had been flown at very high speed brought, on 1 August 1942, a limitation order of 300 mph, embargoes on aerobatics and violent manoeuvres, and a proviso on carrying fuel in the rear tank.

With its penchant for gathering speed in a dive, the Thunderbolt had entered the realms of compressibility, about which little was known at the time. At 500 mph the air began to act like a steel vice, exerting tremendous pressures on all the aircraft's control surfaces, often with disastrous results. By early September, Republic had designed and tested a new metal-covered rudder and this, with reinforcement to the fin, proved completely satisfactory in eliminating tail 'flutter' – hardly an appropriate description as the previous assembly had been subjected to tremendous vibrations in these dives. This was by no means the end of these troubles.

The first service examples of the new model P-47Cs were accepted in September 1942. Even though they incorporated strengthened tail surfaces, a new engine mounting and aerial mast – all of which had proved unsatisfactory on the P-47B – the P-47Cs created incidents. For example, beyond 500 mph, recovery from power dives was extremely hazardous as elevators would not respond because of compressibility forces; in fact, controls tended to be reversed. Use of the elevator trim was the only saving device in such a situation plus the application of power to pull the nose up. To overcome these difficulties bob weights were installed in the elevator control system with the P-47C-1 models that began to appear in late October. Even so, this did not fully overcome the problem and restrictions had to remain until the elevator control system was satisfactorily re-worked.

When restrictions were lifted, it was still deemed

necessary to place a conspicuous notice in the cockpit of Thunderbolts outlining safe diving speeds. This notice stated that diving speed should not exceed 250 mph above 30,000 ft and that speeds could be raised progressively, as altitude was reduced, to a maximum of 500 mph at 10,000 ft. These were safe speed limits but as more was learned about the Thunderbolt's behaviour, so the experienced Air Force pilots advanced possible performance still further.

On Friday, 13 November 1942, Lieutenants Harold Comstock and Roger Dyar of the 63rd Fighter Squadron had been ordered to make level speed run tests in P-47Cs. The first run was at 35,000 ft. After completing this stage at over 400 mph they dived to make another run at a lower level. In a matter of seconds both were in the compressibility 'vice' and the pilots were amazed to see that at one point their air speed indicators were registering the equivalent of 725 mph – beyond the speed of sound! Luck was with them as the badly buffeted Thunderbolts were brought out of their earthwards plunge to deposit two incredulous and rather shaken pilots safely back at their base. In reality, however, the true speed was probably in the 500 mph region because the P-47 could not attain such a pace as 725 mph, its terminal velocity being around 600 mph.

Wright Field engineers ran an extensive evaluation of the P-47C-1-RE and, among their conclusions, they stated the P-47 had the best rate of aileron roll found in any type of US fighter. Latches for linking the engine throttle, propeller and turbo-supercharger controls so that correlated operation could be obtained by moving them by a single lever were a feature of this model. Intended to simplify pilot operation during cruise flight, the Wright Field test team found that it 'gave no trouble'. On the demerit side, one of their chief criticisms related to the restricted view over the aircraft's nose which would make deflection shooting extremely difficult.

The P-47C-2 model was the first Thunderbolt considered to be truly combatworthy. It embodied production modifications deemed satisfactory to overcome the control problems, and also made provision for shackles and a release mechanism for attaching a bomb or external fuel tank to the underside of the aircraft's 'belly'.

Money was no longer an obstacle to the acquisition of warplanes and alternative sources of production were planned for most major models, including the Thunderbolt. The War Production Board had authorised construction of a new factory adjoining the local airport at Evansville, Indiana, and this was scheduled to start turning out P-47s in June 1943. Work on the plant began early in 1942 and through an extraordinary well organised effort the first Thunderbolt was rolled out the following September, with a gala day fly-off on the 19th. However, facilities at Evansville were far from complete and only ten P-47s had been delivered by the end of the year, full production not being achieved until the summer of 1943. First models from Evansville were identified as P-47D-RE and were essentially similar to P-47C-2-RE from Farmingdale.

A third source of Thunderbolts was established through an arrangement with Curtiss-Wright to open a line at their Buffalo, New York, plant. The first specimen aircraft was completed in the same month as Evansville's but production delays plagued this line. Curtiss-built Thunderbolts were designated P-47G and the first had a specification equivalent to the P-47C-RE. As P-47Gs tended to lag behind Republic-built models in regard to the latest refinements, they were assigned to non-combat zones, most aircraft going to US-based training units.

Service testing of the Thunderbolt had cost the lives of 13 pilots and 41 aircraft wrecked. From many of these incidents pilots had emerged very little hurt. The extremely sound construction of the Thunderbolt which withstood the atmosphere loads experienced at 600 mph, also protected the pilot in all but a nose-first crash. Men who had 'bellied' the P-47 in when power failed found that the aircraft did not disintegrate around them with the impact and was often little damaged. The ducts that ran along the bottom of the fuselage between engine and turbo-supercharger acted as a buffer, protecting the pilots' legs. Experienced pilots, conditioned to the hazards of engine failure on take-off and the likely termination of an Air Force career, were soon appreciative of the fact that the Thunderbolt afforded the pilot more protection in such an incident than any other fighter they had encountered.

The P-47 had been conceived and born as a high-altitude interceptor fighter, primarily to meet a defensive requirement, the destruction of hostile bomber aircraft. By the autumn of 1942 the prospect of any aerial assault against the United States was remote and military planning centred on offensive measures. The interceptor fighter would be needed to defend any American land forces sent to battle but at this time another requirement could be met. The Allies had agreed to 'beat Germany first' and as a prelude to an invasion of occupied Europe to reach Germany, a compaign of strategic bombardment from the air was to be pressed. Already USAAF heavy bombers had joined the Royal Air Force in strikes across the English Channel, flying in daylight whereas their British partners flew by night. Although it was thought that large formations of American bombers could protect themselves against enemy interception by means of their massed firepower, fighter support was considered a useful aid to this offensive. The best US fighter for bomber escort and support at that time was the twin-engined, long-ranged Lockheed P-38 Lightning, but limited production, and the demands of other theatres of war where its presence was considered more essential, delayed its availability for units in England. The Thunderbolt was proposed as a substitute. Despite its appetite for fuel — it consumed between 90 and 130 US gallons an hour at cruising speeds, dependant upon altitude — the 305 gallons of the internal tankage allowed an endurance of $1\frac{1}{2}$ to 2 hours under operational conditions. Operating from the UK the P-47 would have a radius of up to 200 miles, about 50 miles more than the Spitfire. Thus the decision was made to send the first combat Thunderbolts to the United Kingdom and to establish a force there for bomber support — the antithesis of the aircraft's original role.

Despite its substantial proportions, the Thunderbolt presented good streamlining when viewed head-on. Extended oil cooler outlet shutters mar the lines of this P-47B. *Below* Thunderbolt firepower. A butts test with tracer ammunition makes a spectacular picture — and also shows the danger from richochets. (Republic)

3 Into the Ring with the Luftwaffe

The first shipment of Thunderbolts arrived at a British port a few days before Christmas 1942. A total of 88 had been deck loaded at New York and despatched to the US Eighth Air Force, USAAF's operating agency in the United Kingdom. Further shipments would follow at regular intervals and it was planned to have enough on hand to equip three fighter groups of three squadrons each to be operational by the spring. Of these one was the 4th Fighter Group which had been formed from the RAF's Eagle Squadrons (units composed of American volunteer pilots) which was to convert from Spitfires, second was the 78th Fighter Group which had come to England with P-38 Lightnings but had all its aircraft and the majority of pilots sent down to North Africa as replacements, and last the 56th Fighter Group whose personnel would arrive in England mid-January. The 4th had experience of operations, and the 56th of the aircraft; the 78th neither. But the ingredients for an effective organisation were there, and it was to be moulded along the lines of the RAF's fighter force. Indeed, USAAF's fighter control, communication and tactics systems were initially modelled on those of the RAF.

Thus presented with this new untried fighter, VIII Fighter Command had to instigate a programme of test flying to obtain performance data and evaluate the aircraft from an operational standpoint, as at that time no such data was available from sources in the United States. The task was put in the hands of Major Cass Hough, a test pilot and engineer for the Command, who spent two weeks flying a P-47C from Bovingdon airfield at every opportunity. At the end of this period Major Hough had amassed a substantial number of facts on the aircraft's speeds, endurance at various powers, rates of climb and other factors which it was vital to analyse before committing the P-47 to battle. Hough had previously tested the P-38 Lightning in England and he held this aircraft in high esteem. Even so he brought an unprejudiced mind to work with the Thunderbolt and found that the more he flew it, the more he liked it.

Despite the stipulated speed limitations for P-47s in dives, within a few weeks of the type's arrival in the United Kingdom there was one fatal and one near fatal dive involving Eighth Air Force pilots. To learn more about the Thunderbolt's behaviour when caught in compressibility, Cass Hough undertook a series of test dives at the end of February 1943 and during one undoubtedly reached the aircraft's terminal velocity.

On the other side of the English Channel two elite Luftwaffe fighter organisations composed of fifteen or so *Staffeln* (squadrons) would be ready to give the new fighter a hard time with their Messerschmitt Bf 109s and Focke-Wulf Fw 190s. It was therefore only prudent that the P-47C should be put through its paces with specimens of these German fighters captured and flown by the RAF. In trials with an Fw 190A the Thunderbolt proved the faster in horizontal flight at altitudes over 15,000 ft. Its acceleration was not up to that of the Focke-Wulf but in a chase it could eventually overhaul the German aircraft and then pull away from it. Lack of initial acceleration was particularly marked in a climb from horizontal flight and even in a dive the Focke-Wulf pulled away rapidly, although here it did not take long for the Thunderbolt to close. The P-47 could turn with the enemy aircraft but the greater agility of the Focke-Wulf soon gave it the advantage unless the P-47's speed could be kept above 250 mph. As the P-47 tended to lose speed in a turn such fights were clearly hazardous. In fact, in most circumstances the Fw190 could out-climb and out-manoeuvre the P-47, leaving superiority in horizontal and diving speeds as the American fighter's chief advantages. Obviously then, in the first instance P-47 operations should be restricted to heights above 15,000 ft, dog-fights avoided, and zoom climb tactics employed in attacking enemy fighters. Zoom climb was the term for a climb aided by the momentum of a preceding dive.

The first P-47Cs were sent to the VIII Fighter Command's training station at Atcham, just outside Shrewsbury. Here pilots went through a conversion course but to expedite matters training was also conducted at Debden (Essex), Goxhill (Lincolnshire) and

Right and Below First Thunderbolts committed to combat were the P-47C-2 and C-5 models; both were refined versions of the P-47C-1 with minor changes. Externally they could often be distinguished by different radio aerials of their radio sets – a rigid mast on the C-2 and a whip aerial on the C-5 – but radio changes were frequently made in service. The examples here were photographed at Kings Cliffe, England in March 1943.

Right A 353rd FG crew chief hand-signals a P-47D-5-RE, carrying a 75 US gallon metal tank, into the desired parking place on a Metfield hardstand.

Left Major Cass Hough and his personal P-47D used for later test flights. *Below* Ground crew 'pulling through' to remove any surplus oil from engine cylinders before starting. A bulbous 200 gallon ferry tank adapted for combat is attached to this P-47C-5-RE (41-6373; HL:Z), flown by the CO of 83rd FS. The wood wedge fixed to the front was to ensure the tank was forced away from the aircraft on release. Flush fitting 'skirt' was fashioned to cover plumbing and smooth air flow.

Kings Cliffe (Northamptonshire), the respective bases of the 4th, 78th and 56th Fighter Groups. At Debden the arrival of the Thunderbolt was not popular, chiefly due to the contrast between the Republic giant and the Spitfire to which pilots were accustomed. The transition was not an easy one, most pilots finding the P-47 sluggish and unmanoeuvrable, as indeed it would appear after experience in the cockpit of a machine weighing about a third as much. At Goxhill most of the pilots were fresh from training on the aircraft in the United States and only the few deprived P-38 men were critical; Kings Cliffe units, however, had a certain jubilation on being reunited with the beast they had come to tame.

The Thunderbolt, alas, did not at first take kindly to its new environment. High in the wintry English sky engines at times would cough and splutter and sometimes cut out completely. The air at 25,000 ft over north-west Europe usually has a far higher humidity than that of the New England area in the USA. In this instance it asserted its presence by creeping into the ignition systems, making it necessary to seal spark plug leads with special damp-proof compound and, at the same time, to lag the engine push rod covers to raise cylinder head temperatures which tended to be far too low.

A certain amount of radio modification and replacement had to be performed so that the aircraft had similar VHF facilities to RAF fighters, but here a new problem arose. Strangely, radio communications with many P-47s were almost impossible due to noise, soon diagnosed as interference from the engine's powerful ignition. A first operational sweep was made by the 4th Fighter Group with 14 P-47s on 10 March 1943 in conjunction with 15 RAF squadrons. Unfortunately the Thunderbolts were plagued by this radio interference and no further operations were carried out until the trouble was solved. Static electricity from corrosion of magneto seals was the principal cause and bonding insulation of magneto distributor caps was the solution, albeit temporary, as the trouble was not completely eliminated until much later with the pressurisation of magnetos.

On 8 April operations commenced in earnest with a sweep by 24 aircraft over the Pas de Calais. This and following operations by the three groups over the next few weeks were chiefly fighter sweeps conducted at around 30,000 ft with limited penetration over enemy occupied territory. The first known brush with Luftwaffe interceptors came on 15 April 1943 and resulted in a brief skirmish between the 4th Group and some Fw 190s. Major Don Blakeslee dived on a flight

of three and was able to shoot one down on the outskirts of Ostend to claim the first victory for the Thunderbolt. Three P-47s failed to return, one shot down in the engagement and the other two almost certainly lost due to engine failure. Two of the pilots were killed, Captains Richard D. McMinn and Stanley M. Anderson, first men to fall in battle with the Thunderbolt.

This opening bout did nothing to endear the P-47 to the 4th Group, particularly as the supposedly reliable radials had failed to maintain their reputation. The next few weeks saw several Thunderbolts failing to return from operations due to engine trouble but the VIII Fighter Command investigating team soon realised that there were many common factors, chiefly blown cylinder heads and that the failures nearly always occurred after combat when full power had been used. The sophistication of the aircraft's engine control system allowed precise adjustment for all flying requirements, but also enabled the unwary to make settings that fed extreme pressures into the engine so that ignition could occur out of phase and damage cylinder heads or pistons. Power into the engine was measured as manifold pressure and it was essential that the pressure setting went hand in hand with the correct engine revolutions. Failure to do this would raise cylinder head temperatures to a point where detonation was bound to occur. The interrelation of turbo-supercharger, throttle and revolutions was vital. When a pilot's attention was concerned with attacking or escaping his enemy, it was easy to unintentionally take some action that would overstrain the engine. Furthermore, such damage was not easily detected and the actual failure might come on a subsequent flight. While pilots could be cautioned against these dangers, a system of automatic safeguards was evantually devised as an aid against high manifold boost.

Modifications were constantly introduced both at the factory and at depots in the United Kingdom. P-47C-5 models incorporating minor changes to components arrived in the United Kingdom in February 1943 and by April the first of the D series was reaching the squadrons. The P-47D-1-RE was outwardly almost identical to the C-5. Internal refinements included a redesigned exhaust gas duct for the turbo-supercharger, changes in the engine accessory compartment, and increased armour for the pilot. One of the most important advances was effected in the theatre, the development of an external fuel tank that would give greater endurance. First use of external tanks, colloquially known as drop tanks or belly tanks, came in late July 1943 when P-47s flew to the German border with Holland and surprised Luftwaffe fighters forming up to attack US heavy bombers. These were flush-fitting, impregnated compressed paper tanks manufactured in the United States with a capacity of 200 US gallons. Changes in atmospheric pressures with altitude meant that fuel could not be drawn from them above about 20,000 ft so, only partly filled, they were employed to take the P-47 up to that altitude before release. VIII Fighter Command engineers under Major Hough designed and perfected a pressurised tank system employing the exhaust from the aircraft's vacuum pump. First used operationally in August the tanks could be retained up to normal operating heights without interruption of fuel flow. Metal tanks originally designed for P-39 Airacobras were the first modified for this purpose and their 75-80 gallons capacity allowed the Thunderbolt to venture 280 miles from base. Another paper composition tank, based on those originally designed for Hawker Hurricanes, was put into production in England and this allowed penetration to about 325 miles. The drop tank was the means of making the P-47 a real, long-range escort fighter.

With growing confidence in their aircraft the pilots of the three P-47 groups were beginning to make their presence felt in the outcome of the vast air battles that raged on practically every occasion a force of B-17 Fortress bombers were despatched to strike at some distant target beyond the Channel coast. The 78th Group had seen most of the successful fighting and on 29 June 1943, Captain Charles London of that organisation shot down two enemy fighters to bring his personal score to five and be acclaimed the first Thunderbolt ace. The account of this action in his squadron's daily diary reads: 'Three Me 109s seen positioning themselves for frontal attack on the heavy bombers. 83rd Squadron, Red Flight, led by Captain London shot at nearest, which began to smoke and one wheel came down. Enemy aircraft remained in formation so Red Leader fired again and it blew up. Red Leader, closely followed by his wing man, swept under heavy bombers and came up on tail of another Me 109, opening fire at 75 yards, and he just blew up too.'

The German fighters were usually instructed to concentrate on attacking the heavy bombers during daylight raids and, unless themselves attacked, to avoid contact with Allied fighters. This policy was their undoing, for with advantage in altitude the Thunderbolts could dive on the enemy as he manoeuvred to attack the bombers, and then zoom climb back to altitude. Furthermore the Luftwaffe, conditioned to

evading Spitfires for three years, had a stock manoeuvre when attacked of rolling over and diving – a Spitfire being soon outpaced. When this happened before a Thunderbolt interception the enemy was a 'gone goose'. An Fw 190 and Me 109 might gain for the first few hundred feet of the descent but the Thunderbolt would soon be close behind and able to follow most manoeuvres the enemy chose. It took a long while for many German pilots to appreciate that one should never attempt to out-run a Thunderbolt; and many never did! The P-47 had another virtue, its enormous firepower. The fusilade of half-inch bullets loosed from a one-second burst of the eight Brownings could be reckoned to bring down the enemy if the aim was good and the range correct. On the other hand, the P-47 itself could take a great many hits, even from cannon shells and still fly on, particularly if attacked from the rear. Many bullet-riddled and cannon-blasted Thunderbolts were brought home from a combat over occupied Europe to give testimony to its robust construction. Luftwaffe pilots came to comment on this thick hide and those with victories over P-47s generally made their kills by deflection shots at the more vulnerable sectors of the aircraft.

The 56th Group, first with the P-47, was led by Colonel Hubert Zemke, not only an accomplished fighter pilot but an astute tactician with keen appreciation of the advantages and limitations of the fighter his group flew. In the early battles with the Luftwaffe the 56th had often come off on the losing end, but by August 1943 it was fast becoming a polished fighting unit that knew how to use the speed and firepower of the Thunderbolt to advantage. From August 1943 it achieved one success after another and its combat record surpassed other US fighter groups operating from England. The first of these major victories came on 17 August when the Group flew to meet the beleaguered Fortresses returning from the first memorable mission to Schweinfurt. The following is the course of this action as recorded by the 56th's historian:

'51 a/c from 61st, 62nd and 63rd Squadrons led by Colonel Zemke to furnish withdrawal escort for B-17s. Group took-off Halesworth 1520 hrs. Landfall in between the north of Walcheren Isle and Hamstede at 1555 hrs at 20,000 ft. Belly tanks released at 20,000 ft at 1605hrs, 5 miles north Antwerp. Group climbed 20-27,000 ft and penetrated about 15 miles east of Eupen. Rendezvous made with heavy bombers at 1621. A turn made to left and group positioned themselves on top of bombers – one squadron covered first box and two covered rear. Approximately 50-60 enemy air-

Right The first 'silver' Thunderbolt in an operational theatre, September 1943. This P-47D-1-RE, 42-7921, had all its camouflage removed to ascertain weight and performance advantages. It is, in fact, the same P-47 used by Cass Hough for experimental flights. The aircraft is fitted with a metal 108 US gallon tank, developed for pressurisation by 8th Air Technical Section.

Above 'Gassin' Up'. A 355th FG P-47D-5-RE being replenished. Filling point, forward of the cockpit, was into the main tank. Drop tank is a 108 US gallon type. *Right* On high altitude escort missions pilots were often 'on oxygen' for two or three hours. Replenishment of the system was made through valve on left side of fuselage.

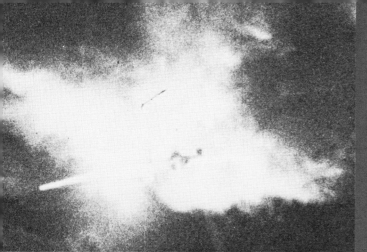

Opposite top A 4th FG P-47C-2-RE with plastic/paper composition 108 US gallon tank built in Britain. These were finished in silver dope whereas metal tanks were painted grey. *Opposite middle left* The P-47 could sure fan lead. An 84th FS P-47D on the Duxford butts, July 1943. Eight .50-inch calibre guns delivered almost 13 lb of bullets per second. Spent cases and links are being ejected on to the hardstand. *Opposite middle right* Servicing the guns of a 78th FG Thunderbolt at Duxford. Individual ammunition compartments can be clearly seen; the outer section of each wing was, in fact, utilised as a magazine! Armour piercing incendiary were considered the most useful round. *Opposite bottom* The *Pistol Packin' Mama*, a P-47D-11-RE of 61st FS, came home to Halesworth after an 88 mm AA shell had passed right through the fuselage without exploding – but evidently damaging hydraulic lines to the tail wheel mechanism.

Above Thunderbolt firepower: the result of a well aimed burst. An Me 110 explodes and the 353rd FG gains another victory. *Right* Cine-camera operated automatically when guns were fired. Cpl Michael Senia of 350th FS installs a new magazine. Camera was positioned behind glazed aperture to the right of cockpit ventilation air intake. *Below right* Lt Col Hubert Zemke, the most famous and successful of Thunderbolt group commanders. *Below* Battle damaged 356th FG P-47D-5-RE with special mount for a Radio compass Direction Finding (D/F) loop aerial behind cockpit. This aircraft was one of a small batch flown to the UK via the North Atlantic ferry route in the summer of 1943.

Top Peel-off into an attack dive by 62nd FS.
Middle Forced down near Caen, France, on 7 October 1943, P-47D 42-8370 of the 355th FG was the first Thunderbolt captured intact by the Germans. It was subsequently flown by *2./Versuchsverband Ob.d.Luftwaffe,* a test and experimental unit, as T9 + FK at Rechlin and Hannover-Wunstorf. A second P-47 (with water injection) was acquired when a 332nd FG pilot, apparently lost, put down near Rome in late May, 1944. (Via Werner Girbig) *Bottom* Luftwaffe personnel examine a 355th FG P-47D-5-RE which came down in a field near the Channel coast on 7 November 1943. Nets draped over white insignia were to hide the aircraft from strafing Allied fighters. (Harry Holmes).

craft seen making attacks on heavy bombers. Mostly Fw 190s and Me 109s plus six Me 110s. A slight change was noted in tactics. Instead of flying parallel to heavy bombers about 3,000 ft above them and coming in for head-on attacks after a 180 degree turn, they were seen to fly at same level as bombers about five miles ahead. Attacks were instituted from this position by making a sharp 180-degree turn and then diving head-on towards the bombers. The Group was able to thwart the majority of these attacks by diving from above on the enemy as they started their dive. As a result numerous combats ensued from the vicinity of Liege to a point 20 miles north of Antwerp where the group left bombers and Spitfires took over.

Selection of Individual Combats.

Captain Gerald Johnson (61st): Captain Johnson had just fixed his sight on an Me 110 and pressed the trigger when he noticed another P-47 had opened up on the same ship. Bullets from both planes played a pattern on the ship. In a fraction of a second the entire Me 110 exploded. Captain Johnson climbed up into the sun, glanced down and spotted an Me 109 heading for the bombers. He dove down on him out of the sun, closed in on his tail and opened fire from 200 yards. The first burst got him in between engine and cockpit. Strikes were observed on his wings and tail. The Me 109 then exploded in mid-air. Captain Johnson spotted another Me 109 coming in on the heavies from astern. He had the speed on him and started to close in a steep dive. He let him have a two-second burst from 100 yards astern, the Me 109 rolled over and headed for the ground. Lieutenant Comstock (63rd) spotted two Me 109s about his level but a little below. As they passed under him he did a half roll and went after them. As he was closing the last Me 109 took evasive action but the first kept right on for the Forts. He moved up to within 100 yards, missed with the first burst (one second) then after correcting his deflection let him have a two-second burst which severed his left wing from the plane. Captain Walker Mahurin (63rd) saw a Fw 190 ready for a stab at the Forts. He closed to 150 yards and opened fire. The whole plane exploded with pieces flying out in a huge smoke ring. He spotted

another Fw 190 between himself and Lieutenant Hall (63rd). This Focke-Wulf was headed for Lieutenant Hall's tail. Captain Mahurin closed on the 190, opened fire, hitting the wing root. The Fw 190 went down out of control. Lieutenant Hall (63rd) spotted a Fw 190 about to make a head-on attack on the Forts. Lieutenant Hall was on the inside of a turn and had the 190 right in his sights. Fw 190 flipped to right and went into spin. Lieutenant McCauley (61st) spotted three Fw 190s in V-formation to the right of the bombers. He dove to attack the right wingman from directly astern. On his first burst pieces flew from both his wings and smoke came out of the right side of the engine, but he stayed in formation. Lieutenant McCauley opened up again. More pieces came off and the pilot bailed out. Lieutenant Schiltz (63rd) broke away from his flight and headed down on a flight of 30 Fw 190s. Two of them must have seen him and turned up to meet him head-on. Lieutenant Schiltz opened up on the leader from 200 yards and let him fly through his fire. Schiltz pulled up to the right and started to circle. Spotting four FWs flying in a string, he closed to 400 yards on the No 2 man and opened fire. At 200 yards he hit the engine and cockpit killing the pilot. He opened fire on the leader at 300 yards with a 4-second burst. His right wing broke off and the aircraft started down. Lieutenant Schiltz circled to find the bombers and found two Fw 190s turning in on the B-17s. He was about 4 o'clock from them. This placed him on the tail of the two FWs. He opened fire on the rear Jerry from about 250 yards. The bullets started to hit on the wing root and continued forward to the engine which burst into flames. Lieutenant Schiltz is the second pilot to shoot down three enemy aircraft on a single mission in the ETO.' The Group score on this operation was 15 destroyed, three probably destroyed and four damaged. Three 56th pilots failed to return.

The Thunderbolt may have been the biggest, heaviest fighter in the world, but in the late summer of 1943 it was fast establishing itself as the most deadly of Allied fighters the Luftwaffe had to contend with at the threshold of the stratosphere.

4 Into the Ring with the Japanese

The second fighter group to commence training on the Thunderbolt was the 80th, which moved into Farmingdale early in June 1942. It received early P-47Bs and for the first few months of its existence operated very much as a source of trained pilots that could be despatched to England. Not until April 1943 was the 80th finally sent on its way under sealed orders. The speculation as to their destination kept personnel busy during the long sea voyage via Brazil, round the Cape of Good Hope, Ceylon and eventually to India. There they found no P-47s to fly and instead of fighting at 30,000 ft the group found itself training again, this time for ground support with P-40 Warhawks. The 326th Fighter Group, activated at Mitchel Field in August 1942, was the third P-47 formation, although it soon became a pilot training unit. Fourth in line for the Thunderbolt was the 348th Group which began forming at Bradley Field in October, training at New England bases until the early spring of 1943 when alerted for overseas movement. Originally scheduled for the United Kingdom the 348th found itself going the other way, destination Australia. In June, 59 Thunderbolts had arrived in Australia for assembly and these were ferried to Port Moresby, New Guinea, site of the main base from which the 348th would commence operations.

The Fifth Air Force, to which the 348th Group was assigned, was a small formation of a few hundred aircraft conducting a highly successful campaign against the Japanese forces. The threat to Australia had been averted and American and Australian forces were pushing up the northern coast of New Guinea, eliminating one Japanese base after another. Air support was vital to this campaign, but bomber missions to destroy enemy airfields had to have fighter escort if losses were not to be prohibitive. The Fifth Air Force's appeal for fighters was met by the 348th and its P-47s, to its disappointment as P-38 Lightnings were required. The dense jungle and wild terrain of New Guinea confined this war largely to the coastal strip and the Japanese had established bases at strategic points all along 'the back' of New Guinea.

Range was vital because these bases, targets for Fifth Air Force bombers, were often a hundred or so miles apart and most at extreme range for P-47s flying from Port Moresby. This was a remote theatre of war with supply problems and the heavy fuel consumption of the Thunderbolt was not to the liking of Fifth Air Force.

Although a great deal of technical data on P-47 combat operations in Europe had been channelled into reports available to the Fifth Air Force, much was inapplicable to its use in the environment of the South-West Pacific. Before the 348th could be sent into action, six weeks were spent by the Fifth Air Force Service Command in designing and constructing a 200 gallon drop tank to fix on the belly shackles, as well as installing an auxiliary feed system. This averaged about 300 man hours per aircraft, each tank being hand made. The results were worthwhile for the extra fuel increased the radius of action from 200 to 320 miles. Attempts were made to get the tank produced in Australia, but various obstacles led to an appeal for a suitable tank from the USA. A shipment of 150 gallon tanks was received some weeks later but these needed considerable modification to instal under the Thunderbolt.

The 348th's first combat mission came in late July 1943 and the Group was soon embroiled in combats with Japanese fighters. The chief types encountered over New Guinea were the Kawasaki Army Type 3 (Ki. 61 Hien), the Nakajima Army Type 1 (Ki. 43 Hayabusa) and the Mitsubishi Navy Type 0 (A6M) – the famed Zero-sen. Because of the difficult designations the Allies allotted code names to all first-line Japanese aircraft and these three were labelled Tony, Oscar and Zeke respectively. A general characteristic of Japanese fighters was their light weight and excellent manoeuvrability, and Allied pilots had learned not to engage them in a turning fight if it could be avoided. This dictated similar tactics to those that Thunderbolt units were employing over Europe; diving attack from altitude and then a zoom climb away. This had been employed with considerable success by

Above P-47D-2-REs of the 348th FG in revetments at Ward Field, Port Moresby, September 1943. A 200 US gallon auxiliary tank is installed on one aircraft. *Inset* The 200 gallon fuel tank with four-point suspension constructed by Fifth Air Force engineers. *Right* Neel Kearby with one of his Thunderbolts. (Via Greg Moreira) *Below* P-47D-15-RA of the 58th FG with white empenage and wing leading edges, an aid to distinguishing friend from foe in the SWPA

Left Settling himself in the cockpit, a ferry pilot prepares for a flight from Eagle Farm, Australia to deliver a new P-47D-16-RE to a Port Moresby airbase. (AFM)

Middle One of the first 'silver' Thunderbolts to reach Australia, a P-47D-11-RA being towed through a Brisbane street to an airfield early in 1944. (AFM)

Left When Thunderbolts with wing racks arrived in Australia, Fifth Air Force was able to extend their range by using P-38 type 165 US gallon drop tanks. The photograph was taken during a flight in February 1944 to determine if the tanks dropped clear on release. (AFM)

INTO THE RING WITH THE JAPANESE

P-39s and P-40s which were no match for the Japanese fighters in a dog-fight. The P-47 with its great speed and heavy armament was ideally suited for such attacks which the enemy could only escape if fore-warned in sufficient time to take evasive action. As over Europe, the Thunderbolt was at a disadvantage below about 15,000 ft where the Zeke and Tony could easily out-climb it. For the sake of performance, Japanese fighters lacked armour and self-sealing fuel tanks and once hit often burst into flames. Japanese fighter pilots were generally skilful and highly trained but their aircraft were designed for dog-fighting, and were thus at a disadvantage in the hit-and-away tactics of their opponents.

Commander of the 348th Group, Lieutenant-Colonel Neel Kearby, appreciating the situation, soon led his men to make good use of the Thunderbolt in bomber escorts and harassing sweeps over enemy airfields. His own prowess as a fighter pilot was considerable and he quickly ran up an impressive score. The most remarkable of his combats came on 11 October 1943. His report on the operation read:

'I was leading a flight of four P-47s on a fighter sweep. We arrived over Wewak at 28,000 ft. The weather was excellent with a few scattered clouds between 2,000 and 8,000 ft. We saw a number of aircraft parked on Boram strip and one aircraft taxiing on the runway. He did not take-off!

'The fuel in our belly tanks had been consumed, so we dropped them to increase our speed and conserve fuel.

'One Zeke was sighted at 8 o'clock below at 20,000 ft. I came in on him from 7 o'clock above and opened fire at 15,000 ft. He took no evasive action, caught fire and dived into the sea.

'We climbed back to 26,000 ft. Saw about 34 fighters – Zekes, Hamps and Tonys – at 10,000-15,000 ft, and 12 bombers, type unidentified, at 5,000 ft, approaching from the east.

'Our P-47s came in from above on a Zeke, opened fire at 1,500 ft and closed as he burst into flames. He took no evasive action. I turned slightly and opened fire on a Hamp at 1,500 ft from 7 o'clock. He burst into flames. No evasive action was taken. I looked up and another Hamp was turning slightly to the left. I closed to 1,500 ft and opened fire from slightly above and from about 8 o'clock. He burst into flames as he passed beyond my sights in the turn.

'The Nips realised we were there, so I pulled up sharply to about 20,000 ft and started for home. Immediately at 2 o'clock below at about 20,000 ft I saw a P-47 with one Tony about 3,000 ft to the rear and another about 3,000 ft behind the first one. I turned and came in at 400 mph on the tail of the rear Tony, opening fire at 1,500 ft. He took no evasive action and burst into flames.

'I closed for the other Tony but he must have seen me and dove down in front of me. I opened fire from about 2,000 ft closing in and saw tracers going into him and pieces of his wing and fuselage flying off. I did not see him catch fire, nor did I see him crash. (Captain Moore, pilot of the P-47 being pursued, saw this Tony burst into flame and crash in the sea.) Tonys were all over the sky. I made a pass at a Tony from about 10 o'clock but deflection was wrong. I looked and saw a Tony closing in on my tail so I dived for the nearby clouds. When coming out of the clouds I could no longer see the Tony. I climbed to 15,000 ft and called the flight. They all checked and proceeded to Lae where we peeled off to land.'

For this action in which he had destroyed six enemy aircraft single-handed, Colonel Kearby was later awarded his country's highest decoration, the Medal of Honor, the first to an Army Air Force fighter pilot. It is notable that all six victims caught fire and the vulnerability of Japanese aircraft to incendiary bullets allowed the Thunderbolt pilot to open fire at twice the range his European counterpart usually needed to obtain a kill. Another factor influencing these hits at long range was the stability of the P-47 when the guns were fired. Despite the heavy armament the Thunderbolt would continue firmly on course when a torrent of bullets was set flowing.

On 5 March 1944, Kearby was shot down and killed by an Oscar pilot when the Thunderbolts he was leading engaged some escorted Japanese bombers near Wewak. At the time of his death Kearby was one of the foremost US fighter aces in the South-West Pacific Area.

Engine failures were the principal difficulties with the P-47D in New Guinea and were probably due to similar causes found in Europe. By and large the aircraft proved dependable despite the difficult debut in its new environment. Minor modifications had to be made, but this was a continuing process throughout the aircrafts' operational life to improve reliability and was, of course, common to other aircraft types. Some unusual engineering matters arose, such as that triggered by a landing mishap. The P-47 had individual wheel brake pedals, and in this incident one pedal became partly detached and fell forward jamming in the pilot's foot-trough. The aircraft immediately veered off the runway and ended up in a drainage ditch. On inspection it was found that a retaining washer was missing from the brake pedal assembly, and it was also discovered that the same washer was absent from the assembly on many other P-47s on the airfield. A report forwarded to the United States brought an inspection of all P-47Ds and it was found that there had been a wholesale omission of this washer during manufacture. The same item was also missing on some older models. All told over 2,000 Thunderbolts had been in jeopardy because of this assembly line error, putting some $233,000,000 at stake to say nothing of the human lives. Happily the omission was discovered in time.

Range problems continued to occupy a good deal of attention, particularly as in some escort missions enemy interception had forced P-47s to jettison their drop tanks at an early stage leaving insufficient fuel to fly all the way with the bombers. A larger internal supply was needed and with considerable ingenuity Fifth Air Force engineers managed to find room for another 42 gallon fuel cell aft of the pilot, by repositioning the radio and other equipment. This fitment, however, tended to affect the handling of the aircraft and was not popular with pilots. Moreover the weight of all this fuel — when drop tanks were carried as well — was more than the tyres could withstand,

especially in the high temperatures. Several bursts on take-off brought fatal crashes and faced with this new limiting factor the additional fuel cell was dispensed with and a maximum load of around 505 gallons specified for safety.

In November 1943, some 300 P-47s were available in Australia and New Guinea and the Fifth Air Force was able to convert some Bell P-39 and Curtiss P-40 units to the type. A shortage of Lockheed P-38s — most favoured fighter, due to its long range — at this time caused a re-organisation of existing Lightning squadrons and two of these were re-equipped with Thunderbolts, one only briefly. The 35th Fighter Group received a full complement of P-47Ds during November and December 1943, and during this period a new group, the 58th, arrived from the United States and became operational on Thunderbolts in February 1944. The three P-47 groups would support the reconquest of New Guinea and follow the 'island hopping' campaign that would culminate in driving the Japanese from the Philippines. Their role, however, gradually changed as the Thunderbolt was found to be admirably suited for duties that were in complete contrast to the original conception. This new role was about to be played very forcefully in Europe.

5 Down to Earth

By the end of 1943, P-47 production had reached its peak, 660 aircraft per month, and throughout the following year the daily average would be over 20. The slow Curtiss Wright assembly line was terminated in March 1944 so that the company could concentrate on expanding production of its C-46 transport. By this date Farmingdale and Evansville were more than able to meet the demand for Thunderbolts for USAAF units and could even begin to arrange supply to Allied air forces who were interested in the heavy fighter. In addition to the New England training area another group of airfields in the Carolinas and controlled from Richmond Army Air Base, Virginia, were busily turning out proficient Thunderbolt pilots, most of whom were being funnelled into new combat groups destined for the Ninth Air Force, newly established in the United Kingdom. The Ninth was a tactical air force specially reformed* as the United States contingent of the Allied air forces committed to support the forthcoming cross-Channel invasion and subsequent land campaign in western Europe. The Ninth received 18 fighter groups during the first three months of 1944, no less than 13 being equipped with P-47s making it the largest user of the type. Next in line was the Eighth Air Force which had received its full complement of 10 P-47 groups by the end of 1943 but was intent on converting most to the new P-51 Mustang which was considered more suited to long range escort. (One group was in fact exchanged for a Ninth P-51 group.) By May 1944, there was a total of 20 Thunderbolt groups in the UK with some 1,800 aircraft making it the most prevalent combat type in operational squadrons on that densely populated 'aircraft carrier'.

The question might well be asked: what was a high altitude interceptor, lately cum-escort fighter, doing in a tactical air force in such profusion? The answer is best given in terms of the developments both technical and tactical that had occurred since the uneasy debut of the Thunderbolt over western Europe.

*The Ninth AF was originally based in the Middle East as a general command for all US air units in that war zone.

The fighter groups of the Eighth Air Force, spearheaded by the 56th Group, went from strength to strength in the autumn and early winter of 1943. As pilots came to be more familiar with the Thunderbolts' peculiarities so they were able to extract better performance from the giant and enhance its value as a fighter. They learned that providing the throttle was kept well forward the aircraft would manoeuvre around a vertical axis in a fantastic manner which few other Allied or enemy fighters could duplicate. Its ability to carry out the 'Split-S' manoeuvre (roll over and make a curving dive to finish up flying in the opposite direction from which the manoeuvre was started) was claimed the best of all Allied fighters. Confidence bore success and time and again P-47 squadrons would return from a mission with high victory claims in combat. In Zemke's 56th Group many pilots were running their personal scores into double figures; men like Gerald Johnson, Robert Johnson, Walker Mahurin, David Schilling and Hubert Zemke himself.

The introduction of locally made 108 gallon drop tanks had enabled Thunderbolts to fly all the way to Emden in North-West Germany in September, and with new groups becoming operational the Fortresses and Liberators were being given continuous cover for 325 miles into enemy territory. Three technical improvements were in the offing and these were to improve and change the situation. The first was water injection, which allowed more power to be drawn from the Double Wasp. A tank holding 15 gallons of a water-alcohol mixture was installed on the bulkhead directly aft of the engine and a line plumbed into the fuel intake. By operating a switch on top of the throttle control the water mixture was allowed to pass into the combustion chambers checking a dangerous rise in cylinder head temperature while manifold pressure was boosted to obtain an approximate 15% increase in power, pushing horse power up from 2,300 to 2,535 and top speed from 406 to 433 mph. The consumption of water was about a gallon a minute and the system was only intended for short bursts of power in

Left Thunderbolts being hoisted from the deck of a merchantman in Liverpool Docks, England, February 1944. In the exposed engine accessories section of P-47D-20-RE, 42-76404 (foreground), the oil tank and pipes for conducting supercharged air to the carburettor can be seen.

Above Special framed trailers were constructed to enable Thunderbolts to be towed through the narrow streets from Prince's Landing Stage, Liverpool to Speke airport where Lockheed Overseas Corporation carried out re-assembly. The P-47D-10-RE, about to start its road ride is 42-75211, which was subsequently assigned to the 374th FS, 361st FG. *Left* New natural metal finish P-47D-22-REs with 'paddle blade' Hamilton propellers at Burtonwood depot, England, April 1944. Camouflaged aircraft have been returned from operational units for modification.

emergencies. Nevertheless, it gave performance increases at lower altitudes that made a substantial difference to the Thunderbolt's rating against its adversaries. Pitted against an Fw 190A, a P-47D with water injection would still not match the Focke-Wulf's initial acceleration but at low altitude – 5,000 ft – this was reduced to a 200 yd initial gain which the P-47 thereafter quickly reduced. In climbs, again the Fw 190 would at first pull away but the P-47 quickly overtook it and then outclimbed it by 500 ft a minute. The P-47 could out-turn the Fw 190 with ease provided the speed was kept above 250 mph. Only when speeds fell below this point was the P-47 at a disadvantage. On these findings and the results of actual encounters when P-47s had been intercepted at low altitudes, it followed that a well-trained pilot in a P-47 could take care of himself. On the P-47D-11-RE and 11-RA models engine water injection was automatically engaged when the throttle lever entered the last eighth of an inch of its travel. These factory installed engines with water injection were designated R-2800-63, and kits were available for modifying the R-2800-21 version of earlier C and D models. Hard on the heels of water injection came the 'paddle blade' propeller which, as its colloquial name suggests, featured wide blades that enabled the P-47's new found power to be used more efficiently.

Third of the engineering advances having an important effect on the employment of the Thunderbolt was the installation of stores shackles under each wing to carry bombs or drop tanks. These, at first attached by depots in the theatre, required a considerable number of man hours, the control mechanism and fuel line plumbing being difficult to instal. To equip every P-47 in the Eighth and Ninth Air Forces took many weeks. For the Eighth this fitment allowed a 108 gallon drop tank on each wing shackle, adding 150 miles to the P-47's range. For the Ninth Air Force it allowed two 500 lb bombs to be carried under the wings and a 75 gallon drop tank under the belly. The combinations were many and gave the P-47 new versatility.

The shackles were embodied in small pylons extending from the under-surface of the wing. They had one detrimental effect in that their air resistance clipped 45 mph off the maximum speed. A redesigned, more streamlined, pylon reduced this loss to about 15 mph.

Back in July 1943, Lieutenant Quince Brown of the 78th Group had been forced to fly his P-47 at hedgehopping altitude over enemy occupied territory on his return from a mission. En route he peppered a gun emplacement and a train. Such action was not officially condoned but from time to time similar incidents occurred. When there were signs that the Luftwaffe was conserving its fighters and keeping them on their bases, orders were given to the effect that pilots could go down to strafe airfields. They needed little encouragement and returning from an escort mission with ammunition to spare, squadrons would 'drop-in' on a Luftwaffe airfield and shoot at any aircraft in sight. It became a very dangerous occupation as the Germans increased anti-aircraft defences which they hoped would act as a deterrent. In March 1944, a special flight composed of P-47s and pilots drawn from several groups in the two air forces was formed expressly to work out the best tactics to use in strafing airfields and other ground targets. The principal finding from these experiments – conducted against targets in France – was that surprise was essential if losses were to be kept low. Airfields, in particular, should be approached from 'zero' altitude so as not to alert enemy gunners until the last possible moment. For this reason a second run at the same target was considered ill advised. Strafing always remained a far more dangerous affair than air combat. Top ranking P-47 aces, Walker Mahurin, Walter Beckham and Glenn Duncan were all brought down by ground fire – but all escaped with their lives.

The 353rd Fighter Group which was host and mentor to the special strafing flight at its base, Metfield in Suffolk, also poineered the Thunderbolt as a fighterbomber in Europe. On 25 November 1943 it carried out the first dive bombing mission, each aircraft involved carrying a 500 lb fragmentation bomb on the fuselage shackles. The target was an airfield in France and the object more of nuisance value with the intention of bringing up enemy fighters rather than to cause any substantial damage to facilities on the field. Bombs were released at about 10,000 ft after a 5,000 ft dive. Not a great deal of harm was done to the airfield – and flak set fire to the main fuel tank of the P-47 flown by the Group commander Colonel McCollom who had to bale out. Other dive bombing attacks followed this inauspicious opening and results improved. The new 353rd CO, Lieutenant Colonel Glenn Duncan and one of the squadron commanders, Major Walter Beckham, experimented in angles of approach and altitude. Due to the difficulty of pulling the Thunderbolt out of a dive at low altitude – it always had a reluctance to divert from its earthward plunge – low level dive bombing from steep angles was dangerous. The other consideration was anti-aircraft defences, so most of these early dive bombing missions were initiated at altitudes around the 15,000 ft mark with

Above and Left Bombing Up. A 500 lb HE bomb being pushed under a 353rd FG P-47D-5-RE on a trolley-jack, which made attachment easy work. The two bomb lugs were attached to the shackle and the four sway braces adjusted to prevent the bomb from oscillating.

Opposite Top In January 1944 adaptor kits for fixing a bomb shackle to the underside of each wing were installed on P-47s in the ETO. Commencing with the D-15 and D-16 these racks were fitted to production aircraft. The refined model on the D-22 is shown with sway braces and B-10 shackle exposed, and with streamlined fairing in place when the rack was not in use. (Aeroplane) *Above left and right* Various lethal combinations could be carried. Here a cluster of 24 × 20 lb fragmentation anti-personnels, or a 500 lb HE with eight fragmentation bombs strapped to it. This kind of ordnance under the 'belly' could prove very nasty in a take-off crash and pilots generally preferred carrying bombs on wing racks. *Right* A trolley-jack being used to lift a 500 lb bomb up to a wing pylon. *Below right* A fragmentation cluster of 20 AN-M41s on a wing pylon. Release vane (forward of sway braces) operated after cluster was dropped, scattering the lethal missiles.

Above Col Harold Holt, CO of 366th FG in his P-47D-20 *Magic Carpet* which set a combat longevity record. The aircraft is carrying a 108 US gallon 'paper' tank and two 500 lb M64 bombs. As the large nose of the P-47 obscured the pilot's view ahead, each pair of fighters is signalled when to start their run by a ground marshal.
Left Due to the restricted visibility over the nose pilots had to 'weave' a P-47 when taxiing. Alternatively, a crew chief would climb on the wing and act as guide. This P-47D-22-RE of the 36th FG is being directed to its dispersal point on Kingsnorth strip, England.
Left The 406th FG assembling at one end of the Ashford, Kent strip for a bombing mission shortly after D-Day. (Russell Zorn) *Below* P-47D-20-REs of 389th FS lined up on a runway at Thruxton, England, prior to take-off. The aircraft were due to escort bomb-carrying P-47s from the same station to a marshalling yard in Belgium, April 1944.

Right Dust fills the air as 42-26066, I7:E of 48th FG prepares to take-off on the just completed steel mesh runway at A-4, Deux Jumeaux, Normandy, 18 June 1944 – the day first elements of the Group arrived from England. *Below* On a French airstrip the 50th FG's *Cyclone Ginny* serves as a clothes horse for these men using steel helmets for their ablutions.

Right Carrying a 'flat' 165 US gallon tank and two M64 bombs, a 373rd FG P-47D-27-RE becomes airborne from the compacted soil strip at A-29, St. James, France, September 1944. (Charles Brown).

Left 'Bubble' canopy
Thunderbolts began to reach
the squadrons in England
early in June 1944. The first
in the 56th FG was used by
Colonel Zemke.
A presentation aircraft
'bought' with war bonds and
named *Oregon's Britannia*
it was given a camouflage
coat of green and grey.
(Via Robert Cavanagh)

Far left Cpt Raymond M. Walsh's Thunderbolt caught up in the explosion of an ammunition filled road vehicle his gun fire had just exploded. Walsh, of 406th FG, and his P-47 survived. The gun camera photo' was taken by Lt Willie L. Whitman, Walsh's wingman, as he started to strafe, 23 June 1944.

Near left The bubble canopy transformed a P-47 pilot's visibility from the 'restricted' to the 'excellent' status. *Maggie V* was one of the first examples of a D-25 to be operated by the 350th FS at Raydon, England.

Left Over rolling French countryside, a 373rd P-47D-22-RE exhibits painted out D-Day stripes on upper surfaces. This photo also shows how the top decking aft of the cockpit tapers and produces the sharp spine that led to the later description of this type as 'razor back'. (Charles Brown)

Right With a battered French chateau as a backdrop, *Warrior Miss* gets maintenance. (Via Ian Mactaggart)

Middle right Fully laden: a checker-nosed 353rd FG P-47D-25 with 165 US gallon drop tank, two 500 lb bombs and six M10 4.5 inch rocket tubes. This view also reveals the large star insignia under both wings- markings peculiar to the P-47 in the ETO and aimed at persuading 'friendly' AA gunners that the aircraft was not an Fw 190. *Below* Combat test installation of 5-inch zero-length rockets on a P-47D-27-RA of 513 FS, 406 FG. Three 500 lb bombs complete the load. (S. Clay)

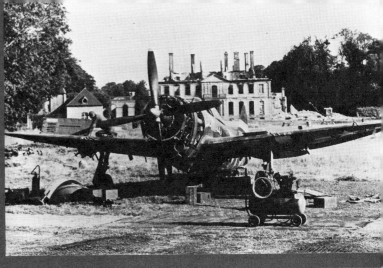

Left Rough. It hardly seems credible but the 358th FG pilot survived this crash (with a broken arm) at Shorne, Gravesend, England in January 1944. (Via S. Clay)
Below left Smooth. P-47D-2-RA, DQ:Q of 495th FTG was put down for a fairly comfortable 'wheels-up' in this English wheat field; August 1944.

Above Most P-47s shot down or crash-landed in France were 'cannibalised' and the remains often left where they came to rest for many months. Here RCAF personnel remove useful and dangerous items from P-47D-15-RE, 42-76207, C2:F, of 368th FG. French civilians — particularly farmers — also found many parts useful. (Russell Zorn)
Left While the P-47's internal fuel tanks offered some protection to the pilot from small missiles, if ignited the cockpit was no place to be. Many Thunderbolts were hit in the tanks and lost through fire. The P-47D-25 with tanks blazing is a 365th FG aircraft shot down by ground fire on 13 July 1944. *Below left* GIs examine a D-22 of 373rd FG that bellied in north east of Beauville. The cockpit section has been completely burnt away by a fuel tank fire. (Russell Zorn)

Above Aligning rocket
launching tubes on a 65th FS
P-47 at Grosseto, Italy. Drop
tank is the 75 US gallon
metal type. Note muff to
keep dirt from entering nose
air intake. Curtiss propeller
has the wide shank
C 38213306 blades. *Right* A
sister squadron aircraft –
64th FS with scorpion badge
on nose – sports a Curtiss
propeller with SPA blades.
These were hollow steel
and composed of welded
sections to a special design
and process of the
A. O. Smith Corporation.

Thunderbolt scoreboards.
Left Lt Col Neel Kearby,
top Thunderbolt ace
in the 5th Air Force. *Middle
left and right* Lt Col Francis
Gabreski (l) and Major
Robert S. Johnson (r), the
two top scoring US fighter
pilots in Europe both flew
P-47s.

Above Sgt Carl Conner, crew
chief, in Cpt Fred
Christensen's aircraft.
Left Major Herschel Green
of 317th FS, 15th Air Force.

Right Cross symbols usually signified the destruction of German aircraft but on Lt Avakian's P-47D they represented sorties completed. The pilot's successes in combat are marked below the cockpit: four bombing raids, two enemy aircraft and a locomotive destroyed. *Below* This display on 362nd FG's 42-26919 includes enemy aircraft, V-1 flying bombs, motor lorries, locomotives, bombing sorties and sweeps. Pilot was Cpt Edwin Fisher. (Via S. Clay)

releases at between 7-10,000 ft.

Another experiment with P-47s featured mass formation bombing from high altitude. Using a Liberator bomber to lead, make the target sighting and give the release signal for the P-47s to drop 500 lb bombs, the 56th Group tried this tactic over enemy airfields. Trailing the slow bomber made this a dangerous practice giving enemy flak gunners an opportune target.

In April 1944 the Ninth Air Force P-47 groups underwent intensive training in the arts of ground attack and dive bombing. The considerable experience of fighter bomber units in North Africa formed the basis of the techniques advised although these were gained with other types of fighter. Glide bombing — steady shallow angle approaches to a ground target — and other modes of attack were practised, and practice was the decisive factor in pilots being able to drop bombs in close proximity to a target.

Most of the expertise in using the P-47 as a fighter-bomber was obtained the hard way through raids on the enemy communications system in France and the Low Countries prior to the invasion. Daily, Ninth Air Force groups went out to bomb bridges, seal tunnels, block railway lines and destroy trains. New methods of approach and of evading ground fire were tried. The evidence of destruction that the gun cameras of returning aircraft brought back told of the effectiveness of the P-47s firepower. The eight .50 guns pushing out 773 lb of bullets per minute could penetrate a locomotive's boiler and disintegrate many a road vehicle. It was quickly realised that the Thunderbolt's guns alone made it a most potent ground attack vehicle.

The Ninth Air Force Thunderbolts really came into their own after the D-Day invasion and the break out of the US Army at St Lo in July. US tanks had VHF radios to enable them to communicate directly with the P-47 pilots and in this way they could call in the Thunderbolts to deal with any enemy tank or gun position obstructing their advance. Thunderbolts flew, whenever possible, armoured column co-operation missions. A flight of four or eight bomb-laden P-47s would circle the leading elements of the armoured column ready to be called into action, while above another flight of P-47s would afford top cover in case German fighters appeared on the scene, which was infrequent. There were occasions when bomb laden P-47s were 'bounced' by Me 109s or Fw 190s at low altitude when losses would ensue.

Ground fire continued to be the greatest hazard and it was necessary for P-47s to patrol above 3,500 ft, beyond the range of the light flak defences of the German army. The ability of the P-47 to take many hits and still fly on was already well known but in fighter-bomber duties the value of this hardiness was truly evinced. The liquid-cooled engines of such fighters as the Spitfire, Typhoon and Mustang were very vulnerable, whereas the P-47's radial could sustain severe damage yet still keep running. Without doubt a pilot's chances of survival were much higher in a Thunderbolt than any other type employed on the same duties. However, while the fuel tanks were well protected by armour plate, if enemy fire ignited the fuel a pilot had to leave fast as the tanks were located directly forward of and under the cockpit.

In July 1944, a new weapon had been introduced on the Thunderbolt. The success of the British air-to-ground rocket projectiles had led the USAAF to experiment with similar installations. P-47s of 406th Group's 513th Squadron (a unit which had the distinction of claiming the first V-1 flying bomb shot down by a US pilot) were modified to carry trackless high-velocity 5-in rockets which were first used against ammunition trucks at Gavray, France, on 29 July. The four rockets (two under each wing) were found to have little effect on aircraft speed or manoeuvrability and were regarded as valuable weapons, particularly in view of accuracy obtained against armoured vehicles. However, in the following month another type of rocket became generally available in the theatre and was less readily accepted. It consisted of three launching tubes slung below each wing directly under the gun compartments and was, in fact, a development of the famous 'Bazooka' infantry weapon. These rockets proved difficult to aim and were not particularly favoured by pilots who considered the installation had a detrimental effect upon performance. The squadron was caught unawares on one occasion by some Focke-Wulfs and four of the rocket-laden P-47s were shot down. Again, practice was required and eventually the rockets were used with good effect against tanks and other armoured vehicles.

While the thousand Thunderbolts of the Ninth Air Force blasted a way across France for the US contingent of the Allied expeditionary force, other P-47s were meting out punishment to enemy ground installations on the Italian battle front. In the spring of 1944 the Twelfth Air Force, charged with tactical operations in that theatre, commenced the conversion of its six fighter groups from a mixed force of P-39, P-40 and A-36s to the P-47D. The mountainous terrain did not allow any startling armoured advances as in France, and it also made the support operations of the air elements far from easy. The P-47, however, was used with effect and soon became popular with pilots and maintenance men alike. The first P-47 group in the Mediterranean Theatre had been the 325th, which began converting to the type in October 1943, and started operations as an escort group in the strategic missioned Fifteenth Air Force early in December. Tutored by experienced P-47 leaders from the Eighth Air Force, the 325th soon mastered the Thunderbolt's idiosyncracies and used it to good account in combat. One pilot, Major Herschel Green, claimed six of the enemy on a single mission and all told ran up a score of 10 destroyed before the group converted to Mustangs. Another group using the P-47 on escort work was the unique 332nd Group, the only Negro-staffed fighter organisation in the whole USAAF. This group too, soon converted to Mustangs which were now favoured for the bomber support role. Advanced German fighter types were appearing and the P-47's performance and range were once again the factors in its employment as an interceptor. Back in the United States however, Alexander Kartveli and his team had not been idle and would shortly introduce a rejuvenated Thunderbolt.

6 Quest for Performance

Legend has it that when asked what he thought of his creation, Alexander Kartveli replied, 'Nice plane. But eet iss *too* beeg'. Events were to prove that any demerit through size was more than made up for by the aircraft's virtues. Size was one thing, weight was another, and there was always a tendency for this to increase as a design evolved. It is understandable then, that having given birth to a colossus, Republic were conscious of the need for restraint in increasing the burden. This in turn led to the consideration of a special lightweight, higher-powered version to bring the P-47 nearer its contemporaries in an unloaded state.

While such a project was reviewed the breed as bred had to be advanced in ways which would maintain its viability in the fighter field without causing serious hold-ups in production. The Army Air Force needed a flow of aircraft to fight the war and manufacturing changes cost precious time.

Republic produced several experimental Thunderbolts, some under a new model letter and others without any Air Force or Company approved designation as they usually involved modification of a Company test aircraft.

Pressurised cabins to provide low level atmospheric conditions at high altitudes, eliminating the wearing of oxygen masks and with attendant benefits to crew comfort, had long been of interest to the Army Air Corps. A pressurised cabin on the Thunderbolt appeared advantageous in view of the fighter's good high altitude performance and Republic were requested to build an experimental aircraft with this feature. The last airframe of the P-47B production run was completed with a pressure cabin as the XP-47E. The installation proved more difficult to perfect than anticipated and XP-47E did not fly until September 1942. Continuing problems with the pressurisation system were not overcome for many months and the aircraft did not achieve successful high altitude flights with the pressure cabin operating until the latter part of 1943. Further trials were conducted at Wright Field in 1944 but by this time the introduction of an 'all-round

view' cockpit canopy on production Thunderbolts put an end to any prospects of a service version of XP-47E.

Another P-47B was taken from production in the spring of 1942 and re-worked to take a special laminar-flow wing with low drag properties in the hope of achieving higher speeds. The laminar-flow wing was developed by the US National Advisory Committee for Aeronautics (NACA) and featured an airfoil which kept air passing over the wing in even compressed layers. The maximum thickness of the laminar airfoil was further back along the chord than with conventional airfoils, resulting in smooth air flow over a greater area of the wing. Designated XP-47F and first flown in September 1942, the aircraft with this new wing offered insufficient advantages over the standard Kartveli-designed airfoil section to warrant further consideration for the Thunderbolt. Indeed, test pilots reported unfavourably on some aspects of XP-47F's flight characteristics. The wing plan form was quite unlike that of the standard Thunderbolt, featuring straight tapering leading and trailing edges with rounded wing tips.

After tests at Wright Field during the fall of 1942, XP-47F was returned to Republic at their Evansville plant. Further trials ensued to obtain data on the low drag wing for NACA. The aircraft was destroyed and the test pilot killed in a crash at Hot Springs, Virginia in October 1943.

Chrysler had a 16-cylinder, inverted-Vee, liquid-cooled engine under development, the XI-2220, and the P-47 was earmarked as a suitable vehicle for flight testing its 2,500 hp designed to be available at 30,000 ft. Like so many aircraft engines development took a long time and the two P-47D-15-RAs taken from the Evansville line in late 1943 to become XP-47Hs languished in a hangar for many months while the installations were effected and the engine ground-tested. So much difficulty was experienced with the engine that not until July 1945, after the cessation of hostilities in Europe, did the first XP-47H take to the air.

While the XP-47H as a test-bed was never a serious contender for the battlefield, the XP-47J showed greater potential. The latter designation was given to the lightweight Thunderbolt version projected in 1942 and approved for a construction contract in June 1943. This aircraft featured a new model of the Pratt & Whitney Double Wasp engine, the R-2800-57 'C' series, with a 2,800 hp rating, specifically designed to obtain higher output without increases in displacement or weight. Previous 'twenty-eight hundreds' used in the P-47 were 'B' series.

The 'C' engine installed in the XP-47J had a special fan to aid cooling which also allowed a more streamlined cowling. A new propeller and improved supercharger were fitted, while weight was saved by structural refinements, reducing the armament to six guns and 1,602 rounds of ammunition (standard D model had 2,136 rounds with its eight guns), fitting smaller fuel cells holding 287 US gallons (as against 370), deletion of all shackles for external stores, and simplifying radio equipment. The aircraft made its maiden flight on 26 November 1943, but after accumulating only 10 hours flying time the engine showed signs of internal damage. A new engine was installed and flight tests proceeded during the spring of 1944.

Speeds approaching the 500 mph mark were being obtained with the XP-47J by mid-summer, with a run at 33,500 ft on 11 July 1944, at 493 mph. With the unattained magic figure of 500 mph beckoning, Republic installed a bigger diameter propeller and a more powerful supercharger. On 5 August 1944 a level speed of over 504 mph at 34,450 ft was achieved, a record for a piston-engined fighter during the war years. However, when the AAF later tested XP-47J at Wright Field, 493 mph was the maximum they could extract during an intensive flight programme and the Republic claim was thereafter treated with reserve.

In any case, these speeds were obtained with minimum loading; when fully dressed for battle the XP-47J's performance was not appreciably better than the more powerful versions of conventional Thunderbolts. The primary reason that the XP-47J was not considered for production was that Republic would have required to change some 70% of the factory tooling, necessitating a break or falling off in production while this was carried out, a situation not acceptable to the customers, the Army Air Force. Additionally, like some of its forebears, the XP-47J had been eclipsed by a superior and more favoured design even before it flew, which also led to the cancellation of a second prototype.

A few weeks after the Thunderbolt's first flight in May 1941 the prolific Kartveli had been busy with two fresh fighter projects utilising new high-power radials from Wright and Pratt & Whitney. That with the Wright (XP-69) was an entirely new concept featuring the radial buried in the fuselage aft of the pilot, driving the propeller in the nose through an extension shaft. Full-sized mock-ups were built but a prototype was never completed due to the Army Air Force favouring the parallel design, which was orthodox, promised a better performance and used many P-47 components. This was the XP-72 powered by the 28-cylinder Wasp Major, rated at not less than 3,000 hp, a thousand horsepower more than the current production P-47Ds. Two prototypes were ordered on 18 June 1943; the first which had a conventional 4-blade propeller flew in February 1944, and the second with contra-rotating propellers five months later. More than 1,500 lb heavier than the P-47D, the XP-72 mounted only six wing guns, and had other limitations to keep its gross weight down. The fuel consumption of the powerful engine restricted range, and the advent of jet engined fighters rendered its top speed of 490 mph unspectacular (although speeds in excess of 500 mph were anticipated when the engine developed full power), bringing about the cancellation of a production contract for 100.

The techniques of mass production were such that XP-72, although very much a Thunderbolt and visually akin to XP-47J, would — as with the latter version too — have been too costly to introduce on the Farmingdale line as a natural progression. Thus the improved versions of the Thunderbolt that did go into production were not radically different from their predecessors. To give all-round vision for the pilot, Republic followed the general trend and installed a bubble canopy on a P-47D-5-RE in July 1943, redesignating it XP-47K. The rear decking was cut and radio equipment re-sited. This bodywork gave the Thunderbolt a much slimmer and more streamlined form.

Another D model became the prototype XP-47L with a redesigned main fuel tank to hold an extra 65 gallons and increased oxygen supply (six cylinders in place of four); other minor refinements were also incorporated. The improvements effected on both XP-47K and L were brought to the production line in February 1944, but a new model designation was not given; aircraft from both factories (Curtiss production had tailed off) incorporating these changes were identified as D-25-RE and D-26-RA which began reaching operational squadrons at the end of May. These new models were some 5-6 mph slower than the

P-47D-22-REs and P-47D-23-RAs they superseded, but the extra 65 gallons of fuel gave an additional 230 miles range, increasing endurance by an hour.

A 30-day test carried out by the AAF's Proof Testing Section at Eglin Field, Florida to ascertain range capabilities and flight characteristics of the bubble canopy P-47, found no measurable effect on turning radius or any significant undesirable traits. This is interesting in view of the not infrequent problem of rudder lock that occurred once the P-47D-25-RE and subsequent models reached operational squadrons. During violent manoeuvres it was possible for a pilot to get the rudder on full lock and be unable to straighten it out again. This was due to the turbulent wake from the bubble canopy with lack of fuselage spine to smooth the air flow. A forward extension to the fin helped to rectify the deficiency in keel area, although both factory installation and modification kits did not reach operational squadrons until late in 1944 and early 1945.

The major steps in extracting maximum performance from the basic design were those connected with advanced power plants. Once the initial troubles with the 'B' series engines (2800-21, -59, and -63) were solved they had proved extraordinarily reliable considering the varied circumstances of their use and abuse. The 'C' series Double Wasp installed in the XP-47J was, therefore, a logical step in bettering the performance of production Thunderbolts. Trials were carried out with the 'C' in Company test aircraft including the XP-47L and during the spring of 1944 four P-47D-27REs were fitted with these engines; three as YP-47Ms, while the fourth eventually emerged as XP-47N. The former were basically test beds for speedy evaluation of the engine and associated components in the normal P-47 fuselage. A more powerful turbo-supercharger and a number of automatic devices for this and engine controls were installed. A General Electrics Unilever control system to automatically correlate turbo, throttle and propeller was also tested but proved unsatisfactory at this stage of development. The 2,800 hp engine, however, gave the YP-47Ms top speeds 50 mph in excess of the 'D'.

Republic were well aware of the Thunderbolt's deficiencies in radius of action, relative to the offensive campaigns to which it was committed. Company representatives in combat theatres were, from the earliest days of the P-47's introduction, faced with frequent criticism from USAAF personnel of the fighter's limited endurance. Various experiments to increase fuel capacity by installing additional tankage in the fuselage could not be taken beyond the stage reached with the XP-47L without severely affecting flight stability. Another approach to the problem was enlarging the wing to incorporate fuel cells. If such a project was to be successful it was essential that the revised structure could be introduced with minimum disruption to production. During the winter of 1943–1944 Republic worked on the most practical solution, an additional wing section inserted between the fuselage and the existing wing. Each section would contain fuel cells for 100 US gallons, raising the total capacity of the P-47 from 370 to 570 gallons and thereby doubling the practical combat range. The location of this additional tankage, being around the aircraft's centre of gravity, would be less likely to adversely affect flight characteristics.

Experimental wing insert sections were first fitted to one of the Company's test aircraft, a P-47C. Refinements brought a further experimental installation, of what became known as the Long-Range Wing, to the XP-47K. These were Republic financed developments, the first official backing for the project being forthcoming in May 1944 when expenditure for the installation of the Long-Range Wing on the third YP-47M was approved. Flight trials of Company test aircraft with modified wings apparently began in June 1944 and the official prototype, re-designated XP-47N, took to the air on 22 July. XP-47N was flown between 1 and 6 August 1944 by Wright Field test pilot, Captain R. B. Johnston, who reported: 'The airplane handles easily considering its weight and was pleasant to fly. All control forces are light. At 400 mph IAS the aileron loads were fairly heavy but not objectionable. The rate of roll seems as good, if not better, than on previous P-47 models. The airplane does not mush as much in tight turns as before. The turning radius appears to be improved over previous P-47 airplanes.'

On this showing of the XP-47N it was expected that this model would eventually supersede the 'D' on both Farmingdale and Evansville lines. Although the first P-47N-1-RE was completed on 16 September 1944 production was some weeks getting into full stride and in the interim it was decided to use available R-2800-57s ('C' series) engines in the manufacture of a small number of P-47M models. The war in Europe was far from over and though the P-47's role there was now primarily one of ground attack, one escort unit clung lovingly to its Thunderbolts. To meet their requirements for speed to match the faster enemy types, the P-47M was put into production. The last 130 P-47D-30-REs on the Farmingdale line were completed as P-47M-1-REs during October/November 1944 and depatched to the United Kingdom.

Right Externally, the hinged canopy distinguished the pressure cabin XP-47E, here photographed at Wright Field in the autumn of 1943. Finish at this time was reportedly a pale blue-grey overall. (Republic) *Below* Construction of the laminar-flow wing of XP-47F in the Farmingdale plant, 25 June 1942. Despite great care to ensure a smooth surface it was found necessary to use a filler before polishing. (Republic)

Right Apart from the engine, XP-47J differed in many ways from production Thunderbolts, noticeably in the turbo-supercharger arrangement which dispensed with the side intercoooler doors in favour of ventral discharge outlets. Spine fairing was cut back to give better rearward visibility. (Republic)

Left First Thunderbolt with a 'bubble' canopy, XP-47K was later used to test a long-range wing with integral fuel cells. (Harold G. Martin) The XP-47H was a test bed for the powerful Chrysler XI-2220 engine which incorporated many novel features aimed at giving high power with minimum vibration. The first aircraft (*below*) flew in July 1945 and the second (*bottom*) some weeks later. (Republic & Harold G. Martin)

Right Several Thunderbolts were retained at Farmingdale for use by Republic in development work. P-47B, 41-5948, became a test bed for a 'C' type engine with contra-rotating propellers, presumably in connection with the XP-47J and XP-72 projects. The aircraft was piloted by C. Hart Miller when this photograph was taken. (Warren Bodie collection)

Middle XP-47N during an early flight. Wing was basically the original quasi-elliptical design with tip clipped and an added section at the root.

Below The ultimate in Thunderbolt development was XP-72. When fully developed its 3,000 hp radial was expected to give the aircraft top speed of over 500 mph. This is the second aircraft with an Aero Products contra-rotating propeller. (Republic)

7 The 'M' and others in Europe

The Eighth Air Force in England had quickly reduced its complement of P-47 groups from ten in January 1944 to four by the following May. Its P-38 groups were converted to Mustangs in the months succeeding D-Day, but not until the autumn was it the turn of further P-47 units to go over to the P-51. In the meantime, the four groups used their Thunderbolts for high altitude escort and ground attack. One day they would play shepherd to B-17s and B-24s five miles above Germany, the next they would be down to tree-top height over France strafing and bombing tactical targets to support the land campaign. The four groups, the 56th, 78th, 353rd and 356th became something of an aerial fire brigade, utilised to meet the needs of other Allied commands as well as their own. The shining example was their commitment to neutralise light anti-aircraft gun positions in the area of the Allied airborne landings in the Netherlands during September 1944. In dull, hazy conditions which hid the enemy, the P-47s had to fly back and forth waiting to be fired at so they could establish the source and attack it. This was an extremely hazardous procedure which brought heavy losses, and the proud 56th suffered no less than 16 P-47s missing on one mission, its highest loss of the war.

By January 1945 only the 56th Group retained the Thunderbolt and was loath to have it taken away. The saving grace was the 130 P-47Ms, then arriving in England, which promised far superior performance to the late model Ds they were flying. The pilots were not disappointed for the aircraft reaching 465 mph at 32,000 ft was faster than the Mustang. On the other hand, the model weighed more than the 'D' due to the engine accessories (100 lb), supercharger (24 lb) and new propeller (8 lb) and some small alterations to the airframe. Operating radius using internal fuel supply could be 300 miles against 325 for the late 'D' models, but with two drop tanks this range could be doubled; therefore the increased appetite of this new model did not really have any appreciable effect on range problems facing the 56th. To send the aircraft through the thin air at speeds in excess of 450 mph with the

throttle fully open demanded a prodigious 330 gallons an hour fuel comsumption, but at cruising speeds the P-47M would average around 100 gallons per hour. Considerable improvement in endurance had been achieved by training P-47 pilots in the technique of cruise control, selecting the best settings to obtain optimum economy on long flights to and from a hostile area.

The jubilation of the 56th at keeping the aircraft with which it had established its fame and thwarting the attempt to give it P-51s, was short lived. Within a few days of putting the P-47M on operations the Group realised it was once again in the position of trouble-shooter for engine malfunction. Worse, it was not just a single problem but many.

The first trouble occurred at high altitude. A pilot would soar to 30,000 ft with the Double Wasp singing sweetly, but the moment he levelled out and reduced power the engine cut. What was more, every P-47M in the group had the same symptoms. The matter was brought to a head on 23 January 1945 when one cut out completely and would not re-start, the pilot having to make a dead stick belly landing on his base at Boxted, Essex. Realising that something was radically wrong with the engines, the 56th contacted the Maintenance and Technical Services at Bovingdon, the organisation specially devoted to USAAF operational engineering problems in Europe. At the same time, the Group reported that engine cylinder head temperatures were excessively low at all altitudes and could only be raised by high power flying.

To Cass Hough, Maintenance and Technical Services deputy director, these troubles sounded very similar to those experienced with the first P-47Cs to arrive in England during January 1943. Consequently, he advised the 56th to look for cracked high tension leads from the magneto to distributor on the belly-landed P-47M. Inspection revealed bad cracks which had obviously led to shorting out. Further cracks were discovered on other P-47M engine leads so a programme of replacement was instigated, the original plastic-covered type being removed and special

i   *Right* Two P-47D-1-RAs
over the New England
coastline in 1942. Coloured
cowlings were the common
form of squadron marking
within a group. (USAF)

ii   *Below* Engine start. A 375th
FS, 359th FG P-47G at
Langley Field, Virginia on
7 July 1943 when this unit
was under training. (USAF)

Left Black and white checkerboard distinguished P-47s of the 78th FG from April 1944. (USAF) *Below* Ground crew working around P-47D-1-RE, 42-7877, HV:D of the 61st FS at Halesworth, England in October 1943. Nicknamed *In The Mood* the fighter was used by Captain Gerald Johnson to make at least six of his 18 air victories. (USAF) *Bottom left* Walker Mahurin, a leading fighter ace with his personal P-47-D-42-8487. (unknown)

vi *Opposite bottom right* A
    veteran P-47D-6-RE of 361st
    FS on dispersal at Martlesham
    Heath, summer 1944.

vii *Top* Red nose and spinner
    was an Allied theatre
    marking in the
    Mediterranean. *Dallas
    Blonde* flew with the 66th FS,
    57th FG. (USAF) *Above*

viii Making a low-level pass over
    the Corsican countryside, a
    12th Air Force P-47D
    commences laying a smoke
    screen. Smoke was generated
    by special M-10 chemical
    tanks slung on wing pylons.

x   (USAF) *Right* The 65th FS
    commander's 14th personal
    aircraft carrying rocket tubes
    and 500 lb bombs on a
    bridge-busting mission over
    northern Italy. (USAF)

Left and below Thunderbolts of the 27th FG photographed in Germany in 1945. Yellow markings were used by 524th FS and red by 522nd FS. Dorsal fin was a "field" modification on both these aircraft. (Unknown) *Bottom* The three squadrons of 56th FG each used a distinctive camouflage scheme on their P-47Ms. 44-21112 was the aircraft usually flown by Major George Bostwick who had 9 air and 6 strafing victories. (Unknown)

xiii *Right* Colourful line up of
      413th FS (yellow) and 456th
      FS (blue) P-47Ns on Iwo
      Jima in the summer of 1945.
xiv   (Unknown) *Below* Warming
      up: a Thunderbolt II of 30
      Squadron, RAF on a
      Burmese airfield. (IWM)
xv   *Bottom* Only remaining
      USAAF fighter group
      operating Thunderbolts in
      the SWPA at the end of
      hostilities was the 58th.
      Horizontal cowl band and
      red striped rudder were unit
      markings. (USAF)

Last operational USAF Thunderbolt unit in Europe was the 86th FG. F-47D-30-RAs of 527th FS in these pictures carried enlarged "last four" of serials on tails. (Col. R.C. Casey)

xviii *Right and Below* In 1948
xix Hollywood produced a
fictional account of the air
fighting in Europe called
"Fighter Squadron". P-47s
with colourful markings were
used for the "friendly" side,
while P-51s carrying crosses
and swastikas represented the
xx enemy. *Bottom* Air National
Guard made use of some 500
Thunderbolts in the early
post-war years.
P-47D-30-RA, 44-33565 was
assigned to 156th FS, a North
Carolina unit. (Lee Gover)

Left Painted up to represent xxi one of the Thunderbolts flown by ace Robert S. Johnson, P-47D-15-RA, 42-23278 was used by Republic for publicity during the early 1960s. The aircraft is now housed in the Air Force Museum at Dayton, Ohio. (Unknown) *Below* 45-49335, xxii one of the six surviving Peruvian Air Force F-47D-40-RAs photographed at Piura, 10 July 1968. (Al Anderson)

Left Caged. Ex Brazilian xxii Air Force F-47D 4109, wearing the insignia of 1 Grupo commander, Nero Moura, is on permanent exhibition in a Sao Paulo museum. (Ian Mactaggart)

Right Shimmering in morning sunlight, a banking P-47M-1-RE of the 56th FG exhibits its dive brakes aft of retracted undercarriage. The dive brakes — or flaps — were to overcome the dangerous nose-down trim change caused by compressibility. (Russell Zorn) *Below* P-47M, 44-21118 on a Boxted hardstand in the spring of 1945. The 63rd FS camouflaged its P-47Ms in dark and light blue on the upper surfaces, and decorated them with sky blue rudder and tail numbers, while the code letters were polished bare metal. This particular aircraft was usually flown by Lt Arthur T. Shupe. (John Keller) *Bottom* To increase loiter time over the battle front these 79th FG P-47D-28-RAs each have three 110 US gallon drop tanks. When 'called down' by the ground forces the targets indicated would be attacked with rockets and gunfire.

Opposite left Flak Happy (veteran of 100 sorties) and friends in the 345th FS, 350th FG. These D-27s are each carrying two 110 gallon drop tanks on wing pylons and a single 75 gallon tank under the fuselage. Tail and cowling flap decor is dark blue and white. *Opposite bottom* Displaying the green, blue and white national markings of Brazil, these P-47D-25-REs were a familiar sight at Pisa, Italy, during the last six months of the war. *Above* A French-flown P-47D-22-RE of GC 2/5 when operating as a fourth squadron to the US 57th FG and employing similar identity markings (yellow bands, red nose). *Right* A wing guide was essential when taxiing a P-47 in conditions such as existed at Luxeuil, France in February 1945. All but the final batch of P-47Ds delivered to the French were camouflaged in olive drab and grey. Roundels were outlined in yellow. (IWM) *Middle right* A bomb laden P-47D-27-RE of 316th FS (identified by white flashes on cowling and fin) taxies out at Luneville, France for a ground support mission. *Bottom* Lt Jorge Taborda of *1 Grupo de Avicao de Caca* (unit insignia on nose) in the cockpit of 42-26771. Back-up ring and post sight is prominent in this photograph.

Left Enemy view of a
Thunderbolt. An aircraft
wearing the red and white
striped tail markings of
86th FG delivers its load
near Bologna, Italy,
1 December 1944.

Above P-47D-28-RE, 44-
19691, of GC 3/3 came to
grief during take-off from
Luxeuil in February 1945.
The right undercarriage leg
was ripped off and the load of
six fragmentation bombs
scattered – luckily without
detonating. Despite the
damaged right wing, this
aircraft was repaired and put
back into service. *Left* The
10,000th Thunderbolt built
served with the 87th FS, 79th
FG in southern France. Here
photographed shortly after
completion. (AFM)

Right Snow dispersal was an unorthodox task that the P-47 fulfilled admirably. The 368th FG kept its runways clear at Metz by taxiing in tight circles and blasting the snow away; January 1945.
Below Ice scene at Florennes, Belgium as 365th FG Thunderbolts take off for a mission in February 1945.
Bottom Good use was made of material appropriated from the enemy. Battered German drop tanks filled with waste oil were used by 36th FG for incendiary purposes. After dropping the tanks they were ignited by gunfire. Aircraft nearest camera has a 'screamer' from German bomb attached under wing tip.

Above Failing to become airborne from its Belgium base, soft ground caused a 'flip over' and the shaken and bruised pilot had to be dug out. The bombs remained on their shackles. *Left* Severe damage to a 367th FG Thunderbolt caused by direct 88 mm shell hit. *Bottom left* Freak hit. An 88 mm shell passed clean through the blade on the Hamilton propeller on P-47 42-28794. This was the sixth time that 19-year-old Edwin Wright's Thunderbolt had been hit by flak in 39 missions. *Bottom right* What other warplane could sustain such damage–as this 365th FG Thunderbolt did in flying through tree tops–yet return safely to base. *Opposite top* Unique P-47 unit in Europe was the 5th Emergency Rescue Squadron which patrolled the North Sea and English Channel. Dinghy pack under wing and smoke markers under fuselage can be seen in this photograph. *Opposite bottom* Special two-seat Thunderbolt used by the 56th FG for attempted airborne radar interceptions over Germany. (AFM)

neoprene-covered leads installed in their place.

Faulty ignition leads could only be part of the trouble and the high altitude cutting out led the Bovingdon engineers to suspect the correlation of throttle to turbo-supercharger regulation. As mentioned previously, incorrect manipulation of the various power controls led to too high manifold boost and engine damage on early P-47s, a situation that was met by modifications and improvements to the system of inter-related controls. The correlation was established in tests at the factory, but when P-47s that could reach 38,000 ft over Long Island were transferred to East Anglia they refused to go higher than 28,000 ft on most days; this was due to differences in atmospheric conditions and temperatures. Corrections had been made on the 'D' models by a new control cam for the turbo-regulator linkage, and experiments along this line were conducted with the P-47M. A programme of tinkering and testing was conducted during the last few days of January 1945 and the first week of February on Bovingdon's own P-47M, 44-21113, acquired straight from the fitting-out depot at Burtonwood. The suspicions were well founded, for it was discovered that correlation was incorrect. Resetting cams and other adjustments allowed smooth engine operation at all altitudes with the desirable power settings.

To raise cylinder head temperatures, lagged push-rod covers were installed on the R-2800-57 engine, a procedure that had helped cure the problem on the P-47C's R-2800-21. Little if any benefit was derived from this, so a special metal baffle was made to restrict airflow through the cowl outlet flaps. This proved satisfactory in pushing up temperatures and also went some way to equalising those of individual cylinders. Non-uniform cylinder head temperatures had been a problem before due to the streamlined shape of the P-47's cowling affecting air currents over different parts of the engine.

While this test work was in progress, the 56th Group experienced a few cases of propeller malfunction. The feathering circuit was shorted by a broken spring. When Bovingdon quickly found a remedy for this, they hoped that the P-47M was cleared for action. This was not to be, for P-47Ms continued to have engine failure – this time internal seizures which caused a number of crash landings and fatalities. The question of burnt pistons, a legacy of the former troubles, or something different was raised. Throughout February and into March the R-2800-57 stubbornly refused to behave; corrosion was discovered and eventually the situation was only resolved by changing every P-47M engine at Boxted –

nearly 80.

The new model did not begin full-scale operations with the 56th until April, when the 'D's could finally be withdrawn. In the last days of the European war the 56th did some good work with the 'M' and on a number of occasions used its speed and diving ability to catch and shoot down Luftwaffe Me 262 jets. The high performance of this Thunderbolt made it very popular with the pilots.

Typical are the views of Edward Crosthwait, who flew with the 63rd Fighter Squadron, and shot down an Me 262 at the end of March 1945: 'When the troubles were finally ironed out the 'M' quickly endeared itself to pilots. Most certainly the finest combat aircraft I ever flew – and there were several, including late model P-51s. The extra power made all the difference and you were no longer conscious that you were flying the heaviest single-seater in the world.'

The 56th Fighter Group emerged from World War 2 as the highest scoring group in the Eighth Air Force with 674 enemy aircraft destroyed in air combat, and also as the highest scoring Thunderbolt group in the whole USAAF. The 56th also provided the two top scoring US fighter aces in Europe, namely, Francis Gabreski who claimed his 28th victim on 5 July 1944, and Robert Johnson who had previously been credited with 27 in the air.

Tactical fighter pilots of the Ninth and Twelfth Air Force did not have such opportunities for destroying the enemy in the air, and the three top scorers in the Ninth, Lieutenant Colonel Paul P. Douglas, Jr (368 FG), Captain Edwin O. Fisher (362 FG), and Captain George McLaughlin (404 FG), had seven victories each. No pilots of the Twelfth are known to have shot down five enemy aircraft while flying P-47s.

Six Twelfth Air Force Thunderbolt groups supported the Allied invasion of Southern France in the late summer of 1944 and then most returned to the difficult Italian battlefront. During a series of missions carried out by the 350th Fighter Group on 24 and 25 April 1945 against heavily defended airfields in Northern Italy, Lieutenant Raymond L. Knight personally destroyed at least 20 enemy aircraft by strafing. On the last mission his P-47, 42-26785, was hit by flak and badly damaged. Knight attempted to nurse the crippled aircraft back to an Allied base but crashed in the Apennines. To Knight went a posthumous Medal of Honor, the only one to a fighter pilot in Italy and the sole award of this decoration to a P-47 pilot in Europe.

One of the Twelfth's P-47 groups, the 324th, never returned to Italy but continued to support the ground campaign in southern France, being absorbed into the new joint US/French command in November, the 1st Tactical Air Force. The French element included two fighter groups equipped with P-47Ds and these units, trained in North Africa, operated through southern France and into Germany during the final days of the war in a similar capacity to the US P-47 groups.

There was also a unique P-47 squadron operating in Italy during the final months of the war, the *I Grupo de Caca* of the Brazilian Air Force, which operated as a fourth squadron with USAAF's 350th Fighter Group and had an average unit establishment of 25 aircraft. Personnel had been trained on the Thunderbolt in Suffolk, Long Island, in the summer of 1944 and sent overseas under the command of Lieutenant Colonel Nero Moura, formerly an adviser to the Brazilian Air Ministry. The unit arrived in Italy on 5 October 1944 and the first five operational sorties were flown on the last day of the month. Most of its missions were dive bombing attacks on enemy transportation system targets and 991 US tons were eventually delivered. Nine pilots were killed during operations when their aircraft were hit by ground fire. Nickname of the unit was 'The Ostriches', based on the comic bird in the squadron badge. Brazil received 88 P-47Ds during the war, equipping another unit at home.

The Soviet Union also flew the Thunderbolt against Nazi Germany. According to records, of the 203 P-47Ds sent via Lend-Lease to the Soviet Union in 1944, seven were wrecked in Persia prior to delivery. However, as to with what success the P-47s were employed by Soviet pilots, little is known. Although information suggests that the Russians considered the aircraft too heavy for their purposes, it is also probable that they were reluctant to praise a machine largely created by a misplaced native of Georgia.

With Germany beaten came the time to assess the P-47's part in this victory. Figuratively, some 86,000 rolling stock items and 9,000 locomotives on the enemy's rail system could be credited as destroyed during ground attack by Thunderbolts. On the roads 68,000 motor vehicles plus 6,000 tanks and armoured

vehicles had been laid waste, to say nothing of 60,000 vehicles drawn by horses – pilots confessed that attacking a horse-drawn vehicle was the thing they abhorred most.

The Thunderbolt had earned the respect of both friend and enemy. Ground crews of the Ninth Air Force had taken the P-47 from one makeshift base to another in the move across Europe and found the aircraft reasonably hardy and easy to maintain. Its durability was considerable and many of the P-47D-15s and 20s that were original equipment when the groups started out from England, were still going strong in May 1945. One outstanding example was 42-76516, *Magic Carpet* flown by the commanding officer of the 366th Fighter Group. In 175 sorties it never once turned back through mechanical trouble. Some of the original P-47Cs that had equipped the first Thunderbolt Group in England were also still flying, having put in hundreds of hours on training duties with the 495th Group at Atcham.

Some 30 machines, retired from combat, were equipped to carry air/sea rescue equipment and employed as patrol aircraft over the North Sea. Others were assigned to target towing and special fast communications work. Towards the end of hostilities practically every P-47 group in Europe had one or two machines adapted to carry a passenger. The two-seat conversions were made by the removal and repositioning of radio equipment and oxygen supply, cutting away the fuselage directly aft of the pilot and fitting a seat with the necessary stress members. The canopy took various forms. In most cases it was an extension of the original hood with a hinged section to allow the passenger access. These two-seat P-47s were chiefly used for local flights but in some instances they flew on combat missions carrying an observer.

During the last days of the war in Euope a few P-47N models arrived in the United Kingdom and were being made ready for operational squadrons when hostilites ceased. They were not long in being shipped out again, for this longer-ranged Thunderbolt was needed to finish the fight against Japan.

8 Burma and Beyond

After the USAAF, the largest operator of Thunderbolts in World War 2 was the Royal Air Force. Over 800 P-47Ds were allocated to the British under Lend-Lease terms and most of these were delivered direct to the South-East Asia theatre.

By the time the first production Thunderbolts began to come off the Farmingdale line the RAF had been flying combat operations with many aircraft types stemming from the American aviation industry. They were impressed by the usually sound design and construction of these aircraft, even if some were wanting in performance and other respects. The British Air Ministry had kept its eye on the P-47's progress from an early date and on 26 May 1942, it was arranged for one of their test pilots to fly a P-47B.

At this time the Thunderbolt was offered as a high altitude interceptor and while the RAF had no requirement for such an aircraft, they were well enough impressed by this early evaluation to negotiate an order. They saw the P-47 as a useful offensive fighter but undoubtedly they were influenced in their eventual employment of the type by the success of the USAAF in promoting the P-47, first in an escort role and then as a tactical fighter.

The first 240 Thunderbolts consigned to British service were from the D-22 series and they became Thunderbolt Mk Is in the RAF. Two aircraft (FL849 and FL844) was evaluated in the UK and used for experimental work with drop tanks at Boscombe Down, but most were shipped from the USA to India and when assembled flown to No 1670 Conversion Unit at Yelahanka (near Bangalore) where squadrons were withdrawn from the front to convert. First squadron to receive the Thunderbolt I was No 135 (which began conversion in May 1944) although No 261 beat it to operations by flying the first RAF Thunderbolt sorties, a reconnaissance, on September 14. However, shortages of spares and special tools delayed progress with working up squadrons to operational status. Many Thunderbolt IIs, the 360° vision bubble canopy version, arrived in June, and the supply of trained pilots and aircraft was sufficient to

see nine RAF squadrons in action by the end of the year (Nos 5, 30, 79, 123, 134, 135, 146, 258 and 261). Squadron establishment was 16 aircraft. Nearly all these squadrons had previously been employed in ground support operations for the British 14th Army and they continued in this role with the Thunderbolt.

Flights of Thunderbolts were frequently despatched on 'cab rank' patrols, and when called on by the Army they would descend to attack the offending Japanese target — tactics similar to those used by Allied fighter-bombers in Europe. Moderate angle dive-bombing, usually with 500 lb bombs, was carried out from 8,000 ft with a pull-out at 1,500 ft. Other types of operations for the Thunderbolts were strafing attacks on enemy airfields and escorts, chiefly for cargo carrying Dakotas supply-dropping to forward troops. Even without weapons the Thunderbolt could be useful. For one period of 48 hours during the march in Mandalay the Japanese artillery was silenced after Thunderbolts had dived over the enemy defences to indicate the gun positions to B-25 Mitchells which then blasted the heavy artillery out of action with bombs. Air combat with Japanese aircraft was infrequent and usually on a small scale, besides which the Japanese were generally good at evasive tactics. A typical instance is the bombing raid of 13 December 1944 when Liberators with Thunderbolt escort attacked rail bridges at Mokpalin and Hninpole. The lower cover of Thunderbolts went down to attack anti-aircraft positions and the higher elements descended to between 12 and 18,000 ft to give them cover. The latter were then 'jumped' by about ten Nakajima Oscars. The Thunderbolts dived to 10,000 ft to evade them while the enemy aircraft tried to get on their tails. A series of indeterminate combats followed without loss to either side. The Oscars then made off but encountered a third section of Thunderbolts. Although this time the Thunderbolts had the advantage, the Oscars' caution and good evasive action saw only a 'probably destroyed' and a 'damaged' claim made against them.

The pace of offensive operations increased early in 1945 and as the front moved into Burma the Thunder-

Right The first example of a Thunderbolt Mk I sent to the UK was used for type evaluation. USAAF serial was 42-25792. (British Official) *Middle* A Thunderbolt Mk II after check-out at Farmingdale. This aircraft was laid down as P-47D-30-RE, 44-20506. Wing pylon front fairing had to be removed to locate tie-down point. (Harold G. Martin) *Below left* Colourful red and white checkerboard cowl markings that adorned 258 Squadron's aircraft were short-lived and replaced by official white type identity bands. Wing provided shade from burning sun.(IWM) *Below right* A 22 Squadron Thunderbolt Mk II circles Mount Poppa, a distinctive landmark in central Burma. (Via Jim Double)

Right Thunderbolt IIs of 30 Squadron on patrol over Burma.

Left Flt/Sgt Standish-Walker climbing into a 135 Sqn Thunderbolt. Jungle knife and screwdriver are part of survival kit attached to pilot, which varied according to individual preference. Note push-in toe hold to facilitate access to the cockpit. Push-out hand hold can be seen behind pilot's leg. (IWM)

Below A 79 Sqn 'T-Bolt' on a Burmese strip. The Thunderbolt is believed to have had the lowest loss/sortie rate of any WW 2 RAF combat aircraft: only seven were known to enemy fire (AA) and the total MIA was 15. (Ken Sumney)

Below middle Overhaul of an 81 Sqn. Thunderbolt Mk II at Kemajoram, Batavia in late 1945. Removal of lower cowling exposes supercharger-intake duct and oil coolers. (British Official)

Bottom The first three P-47D-15-RAs of 33rd FG to arrive at Kunming, China, 20 April 1944 after the flight from India.

bolt squadrons often found they had to fly 200 miles or more to a target. Metal drop tanks, classified as 75, 100 and 150 Imperial gallons, were used to extend ranges and some of these were manufactured in the theatre. Another squadron, No 34, became operational in March and another started conversion. In April some squadrons were assigned to Operation *Dracula*, the assault on Rangoon. After this the weather took a hand in curtailing operations as the monsoon broke and airfields became so muddy that take-off was often impossible even if the weather had allowed flying.

Most RAF pilots came to Thunderbolts from Hurricanes and Spitfires and their opinions of the US aircraft tended to be based on comparisons with the British fighters. The good points can be summed-up as follows: Excellent flight stability, which made formation flying no problem and also allowed more accurate attack dives on targets. Dive-bombing accuracy with the Thunderbolt was much higher than with other types of fighter used in Burma. At high altitude its handling characteristics did not deteriorate appreciably even above 30,000 ft, whereas a Spitfire tended to become rather unstable at 25,000 ft. The aircraft also had no vices in take-off and landing, while the wide track undercarriage gave good ground stability that was advantageous on some of the rough strips from which operations were flown. Range was another good feature and 1,000-mile, 5-hour flights were possible.

Merlin engines were dogged with coolant leaks and other problems in tropical climates, so the comparatively trouble-free Pratt & Whitney radials were soon approved of, many pilots considering them the most reliable aero-engines they ever flew behind.

The cockpit was much favoured as it provided plenty of room for the bulky jungle survival gear that was attached to a pilot. To Flight Lieutenant Jack Knight of No 134 Squadron: 'Sitting in the cockpit was a revelation. One immediately felt rather like Charles Smart (popular British entertainer) at a cinema organ, not only because of the vast array of dials and switches, but the spaciousness of the cockpit itself. Both the Spitfire and the Hurricane seemed to be built around the pilot — one could almost do physical jerks in the Thunderbolt.'

RAF pilots were equally in agreement on the Republic's shortcomings. The fat fuselage and large nose made taxiing difficult and was best accomplished by a zig-zagging movement which allowed a view forward over the wing. There were several taxiing accidents and two Thunderbolts were badly damaged

at No 8 Refresher Flying Unit while taxiing along their strip: the first pilot stopped and the following pilot, having his attention momentarily diverted by a jamming tailwheel, ran down his leader. Very long take-off runs — a mile in some conditions — contrasted with the short hops of the Spitfire. High landing speed, in the order of 150 mph on approach and rounded out at 120 mph with power to prevent too rapid a rate of descent contrasted with Spitfires using glide approach techniques with engine fully throttled back. There is, however, evidence of a safe glide-in with a Thunderbolt. Fifteen minutes after take-off for a cross-country flight on KL176, the pilot noted the oil temperature building up and turned back to base. About two miles from Yelahanka the oil pressure failed completely and the engine subsequently seized solid, yet the pilot made a successful forced landing on the strip, wheels and flaps down.

The Thunderbolt's poor rate of climb and poor rate of turn were, however, the chief complaints. Flight Sergeant Ron Capewell of No 135 Squadron once had a Liberator turn inside him during low speed simulated interception! Nevertheless, RAF pilots soon came to appreciate the hardiness of the Thunderbolts and with trained pilots fatal accidents and losses were few. One squadron lost only one pilot in six months intensive operations with the type. Like their USAAF colleagues, RAF fliers also realised that if one was going to be involved in a crash, a Thunderbolt was about the best aircraft to be in. During a night operation by 615 Squadron from Akyab during the summer of 1945, a Thunderbolt piloted by Flight Sergeant Hutchinson failed to become airborne through lack of power and crashed off the far end of the runway. His absence was not noted until the squadron had assembled in formation and Hutchinson failed to appear in his allocated position. The leader immediately informed ground control who concluded that the missing aircraft had crashed. A crash tender was despatched up the airstrip and had not gone far when a figure was observed in the gloom. The crew stopped and enquired if the stroller had heard or seen a crash and if so where. The undoubtedly graphic reply is not recorded, but this was Hutchinson who having extracted himself unscathed from the wreckage of his fighter, and finding no help forthcoming, had set off back down the airstrip on foot.

As in Europe with USAAF P-47s, special white recognition bands were applied to RAF Thunderbolts in the Far East with the object of preventing attacks by Allied pilots who mistook them for Japanese types. On one occasion a flight of No 134 Squadron was vectored to intercept six-plus Japanese fighters converging on Cox's Bazaar, SE of Chittagong. The leader of the Thunderbolts kept a large circuit round the area looking frantically for the enemy aircraft which he was constantly being told were now actually over Cox's Bazaar. Spitfires appeared above which were presumed top cover. The Thunderbolt pilots' comfort through having top cover was short-lived as the Spitfires came down on them with 'cannon ports twinkling.' Apparently the ground observer posts for raid reporting had identified and plotted the Thunderbolts as Japanese fighters.

Some of the final batch of Mk IIs were left in natural finish, in which case recognition bands were black to contrast. At least four RAF Thunderbolt IIs were evaluated in the United Kingdom, including the first of the order, HD182, and the last, a P-47D-40-RA, KL887.

The RAF encountered few mechanical difficulties with its Thunderbolts. Late Mk IIs featured the new paddle-blade Curtiss Electric propellers which, supposedly, had both operational and installation advantages over the Hamilton Hydromatic type and had been re-introduced into production with the P-47D-28-RE. They proved exceedingly troublesome, principally through the damp, humid environment of Burma affecting electrical contacts, the USAAF experiencing similar difficulties.

An unpleasant and mysterious manifestation saw a few Thunderbolts exploding during dive bombing attacks. An explanation was eventually found in ruptured fuel tanks from which fuel vapour seeped into the supercharger ducting, ignited and disintegrated the aircraft.

In the summer of 1945, No 60 Squadron was the last RAF squadron to go over to Thunderbolts, and three of the existing squadrons had a change of number designation – as was the occasional whim of authority. Operations, however, were limited by the scarcity of targets and then the cessation of hostilities brought rapid disbandment of most units. Only Nos 60 and 81 Squadrons remained and these later played a part in the Dutch East Indies troubles with Indonesian patriots. On 1 November 1945, three Thunderbolts on offensive reconnaissance over Magelang area of Java went into action, the first such RAF sorties since hostilities against the Japanese ceased. Four lorries were amongst targets strafed but results were unobserved. Similar incidents occurred over the next few months until British participation ceased. On a number of occasions Thunderbolts of No 60 squadron dropped news and propaganda leaflets from their wing shackles.

In addition to the RAF units, the USAAF had eight P-47-equipped squadrons operating on the Burma front at one time. The 80th Fighter Group, second unit trained on the P-47B but sent to India and given P-40s, finally received Thunderbolts in the spring of 1944. Its duties were much along those of its RAF counterparts although it spent a good deal of time protecting the busy C-46 and C-47 air lines to China 'over the Hump'.

The Japanese were well aware of the dependence of Allied ground forces on supplies from the air and were very adept at making sneak attacks upon the transports. During one such interception on the afternoon of 14 December 1944, a P-47 used its ability to execute violent vertical manoeuvres to evade its pursuers with an unusual outcome. Nine C-47s supply-dropping to British troops on the Bhamo–Namhkam road were intercepted by a dozen Nakajima Tojos (Ki.44 Shoki), which were in turn attacked by the escorting P-47s. Two Tojos were quickly destroyed but not before a C-47 had been shot down and five others damaged. During the dog-fight that followed two Tojos used their low altitude advantages in climb and turning to get on the tail of one Thunderbolt. The American pilot, aware of his predicament, executed a 'vertical reverse' which the Tojos attempted to follow but collided with one another. Both were seen to come apart in mid-air.

When the Allies were established firmly in Italy the USAAF found that it had a surplus of fighter groups in the Mediterranean and despatched two, the 33rd and 81st to India where they were to train on Thunderbolts and defend Boeing B-29 Superfortress forward bases being established in the Chengtu area of China. The two groups found that they also had to help assemble the Thunderbolts which arrived by ship at Karachi, India at the end of March 1944. Removal of the heavy coatings of protective cosmoline proved an arduous and unpopular task, but within a week the first conversion flights were being made. The pilots, who had previously flown P-39s and P-40s in the Mediterranean war zone, were not happy with the Thunderbolts but the ground crews, benefiting from easier maintenance, 'liked it to a man'.

After 30 hours flight time the pilots ferried their aircraft across India and into China to join the Fourteenth Air Force. Here the P-47 was considered highly undesirable for its defensive task. Prejudice played a part, even to the extent that some P-40s were acquired and operated in preference by pilots of the 33rd Group. The Thunderbolt's thirst was a major reason for the type's unpopularity in a war zone where

Above A 91st FS P-47D-15-RA overshoots at a Chinese airfield. Like all Thunderbolts assigned to the theatre a D/F aerial is installed. *Right* The 80th FG had been the second group to train on P-47Bs in 1942 but when committed to combat flew Curtiss P-40s for several months before receiving Thunderbolts. This P-47D-23-RA was assigned to the Group's 90th FS. (Ken Sumney)

Above A distinctively marked (five diagonal blue stripes) P-47D-23-RA of 1st Air Commando Group takes off from a Burmese air strip. When the P-47's undercarriage retraction cycle began the main struts telescoped by about 9 ins to facilitate stowage in the wing. *Right* 500 lb HE bombs being delivered to 1st Air Commando Group P-47D-23-RAs at Hay, India, 10 February 1945.

supplies of fuel had to be delivered by air, and a decision was soon taken by high command to reduce this force. In September 1944 the 33rd Group returned to India, having been exchanged for a group of far-ranging Mustangs. The 33rd's Thunderbolts had seen little activity in China apart from losing the first P-47 to enemy action in that country when one was destroyed on the ground at Liengshan by bombing. One of the 81st Group's squadrons returned to India too, where it became an operational training and back-up unit for the other two squadrons which remained in China until the end of the hostilities. When the B-29s were transferred from China and India early in 1945 the 81st's Thunderbolts went over to the ground attack role. The 33rd Group spent the rest of the war in Burma flying ground support missions until the capture of Rangoon and the monsoon brought a halt.

The other two squadrons were the 5th and 6th Air Commando (Fighter), units of the 1st Air Commando Group, an organisation originally established to give air support to General Wingate's raids behind the Japanese lines. The Group at one time included bomber, fighter, liaison and transport elements, but after re-organisation into squadrons during the summer of 1944 it lost the bombers and became principally involved in forward support of troops. The two fighter squadrons which converted to the P-47 from P-51As were often despatched on separate ground attack strikes. In May 1945, however, these two units reverted to the Mustang which was more suited to their purposes involving the use of small forward landing strips.

A notable feature of many USAAF P-47Ds flying in the CBI (China-Burma-India) theatre was the addition of a direction finding loop aerial. The vastness of the territory over which operations were conducted, and the limited ground radio control in some places made this installation of great value.

While the Thunderbolt's employment in the China-Burma-India theatre was never as impressive as in other combat areas its record was still good. However, what was probably the best individual performance of any Thunderbolt anywhere belongs to one that operated in Burma. Nicknamed *Avis*, this P-47D of the 80th Fighter Group flew 329 combat missions totaling 912 hours and had been hit by enemy ground fire, the most serious damage incurred being when the tail wheel was shot away over Hosi in January 1945. During this exceptional service the engine and fuel pump had to be changed, but the majority of the original accessories were still with *Avis* when her crew chief, S/Sgt Warren C. Jones and his assistant, Sgt Layl C. Bonstead, had to despatch her to a salvage depot in September 1945.

9 The 'N' and the War in the Pacific

When Germany was defeated in May 1945, the United States air forces engaged with the Japanese in the south-west and central Pacific areas included only two fighter groups with P-47s. In the Fifth Air Force, the 58th alone remained of the three groups that had flown the type during the long and difficult liberation of New Guinea and the Philippines, the 35th and 348th Groups having converted to P-51 Mustangs. A fourth squadron had been attached to the 58th Group in 1945, the 201 *Escuadron Aereo de Pelea* of the Mexican Air Force. This unit, under General P. A. Antonio Cardenas Rodriguez, had been trained in the USA on the Thunderbolt and, equipped with P-47Ds, the 201 EAP saw action in the last stages of the campaign on Luzon having arrived in the Philippines in May 1945. Later it moved with the 58th to Okinawa and operated chiefly against Kyushu, the southernmost island of Japan. Like the other squadrons of the 58th Group the Mexican P-47s were flown almost exclusively in a ground-attack role; its war record comprised 96 combat missions during which seven pilots were lost. The squadron returned to Mexico towards the end of 1945 and was split up to share in other units the experience gained. Its P-47s were left in the Pacific, but the US Government made 25 P-47s available to Mexico to replace them.

The other Thunderbolt group was the 318th, a unit of the Seventh Air Force functioning in the central Pacific area, which had literally been catapulted into action in June 1944. The Group was formed in 1942 for the air defence of Hawaii and its early days were spent in training and flying patrols. It received P-47Ds early in 1944. In June that year US forces opened a campaign to secure the Marianas Islands for the building of bases from which strategic bombers (B-29 Superfortresses) could operate against the Japanese homeland some 1,500 miles distant. The first island invaded was Saipan. To ensure prompt air support for the ground troops it was decided to transport the P-47Ds of the 318th to the first available captured airstrip. After flying from their station at Bellows Field, Hawaii, to an airfield that adjoined the dock at Ford Island naval base, the 71 P-47Ds were hoisted by crane aboard two escort-type aircraft carriers. The carriers sailed on 5 June, refuelling at Eniwetok and reaching the Marianas in the middle of the month, where four Japanese bombers unsuccessfully attempted to bomb them. During 22 to 24 June all the P-47s were safely catapulted from the carrier decks – the only such occasion for Thunderbolts apart from experimental trials. This was only a week after the invasion, with some enemy positions still within sight of the Group's airstrip. The 318th engaged in support missions which, typically, would entail one flight strafing a Japanese gun position either to kill the gunners or drive them to cover, and so allowing a following flight to glide-bomb the position unmolested. One Thunderbolt met its end in an unusual way: on the night of 26 June several Japanese soldiers broke into the airstrip perimeter, one managing to get to a P-47 and set fire to it.

During the summer of 1944 the Group supported the invasions of Tinian and Guam, other islands in the Marianas chain, and later when range problems limited its activities with the P-47D, acquired some P-38s and flew missions to other island groups in the central Pacific still under Japanese occupation. By the spring of 1945, however, USAAF had plans to establish a small fighter force equipped with the new P-47N on island bases even closer to Japan. In April, the pilots of the 318th collected the first of these and flew them by stages over a total of 4,100 miles to the recently captured Ie Shima, three miles off the coast of Okinawa and 325 miles from the Japanese homeland.

P-47Ns came into full production at Farmingdale during December 1944 and all 'Ns' to see action in the Pacific War came from this factory. Evansville did not go over from 'D' to 'N' models until the end of the war and only 149 were completed before the contract was cancelled. Although the principal reason for introducing this model was to better endurance, by the provision of integral wing tanks to hold an extra 200 US gallons, the 'N' had a number of other refinements. As previously mentioned, the R-2800-57 Double Wasp that had given the 56th Fighter Group trouble in the P-47M, provided the power. Like earlier 2800 models, once the initial difficulties had been overcome — and these were all connected with control mechanisms — it proved an extraordinarily reliable and durable engine. Like the 'M', the 'N' featured higher output General Electric turbo supercharger (CH-5 model) and associated items. Designed for long range and flights that with drop tanks could last 10 hours, much was done to alleviate pilot fatigue. The C-1 Automatic Engine Control (AEC) gave sequential operation of throttle, turbo-supercharger and water injection. Once the pilot selected a power setting the AEC automatically maintained the setting through changes in altitude and aircraft attitude. A General Electric autopilot system took the strain from pilots on long to-and-from target flights which could involve several hundred miles. The P-47N, in fact, was a much simpler aircraft to fly than previous Thunderbolt models and, in consequence, less demanding of a pilot.

The square cut wing tips were the distinguishing feature of the 'N' and added another 18-in in span and 22 sq ft in area. Four inter-connected fuel cells were installed near the root in each wing, giving the aircraft half as much fuel as the 'D' model. Provision was made for 10 underwing 5-in rockets on flush-fitting installations, similar to the British type, with the N-5-RE series. The 'N' also featured a wider tread undercarriage, a matter of some 24 in extra. All these additions meant the inescapable problem of weight coming to the fore again. While empty this amounted to an extra 1,000-odd pounds advance over the P-47D, but even so handling characteristics were not markedly different from the earlier model. Once the full complement of fuel was aboard and drop tanks, bombs or rockets slung from the wing and belly shackles, the 'N' could gross 20,700 lb, an all-time high for a piston-engined, single-seat fighter.

The increase in weight of the P-47N over the P-47D was soon appreciated by the men of the 318th Group, who needed on average another 800 ft to get airborne. Once at altitude, the 'N' had about a 30 mph gain on top speed. Manoeuvrability was generally not so good, although from a practical point of view insufficient to affect the machine's value in fighter versus fighter combat in the mode of attack practised against Japanese adversaries. The diving attack and zoom climb away still held good as the prudent method of combat with a more manoeuvrable opponent, and like its predecessors, this Thunderbolt's speed could usually be relied upon to get it out of a tight spot.

There were, naturally, occasions when speed wasn't available. A unique incident occurred as an outcome of one such lack of power on 10 June 1945 when a squadron of the 318th was sweeping over Kyushu. Seven unwary Zekes observed below were destroyed in a near perfect surprise attack. Second Lieutenant Robert J. Stone claimed two but on seeking altitude again he discovered his P-47N's engine would not give full power. At this crucial moment more Japanese fighters hove in sight and, noting Stone's sluggish Thunderbolt, prepared to stop it completely. Stone did what many a pilot before had done in such circumstances, dived for the deck. At paddy-hopping height the aircraft presented an extremely difficult target to its pursuers, an almost impossible one if the course was erratic and Stone ensured that it was. The two Zekes close behind occasionally fired bursts which fortunately missed their target. After skimming the top of a hill, Stone suddenly found himself approaching an airfield and converging on a twin-engined aircraft rising from the runway almost dead ahead. Instinctively, Stone pulled the P-47 up into a left-hand climbing turn in the hope of missing the Japanese aircraft. An explosion rocked the Thunderbolt and Stone's immediate reaction was to believe his manoeuvre unsuccessful. Then to his amazement he caught sight of the flaming remains of aircraft on the ground behind his still flying Thunderbolt. There was no sight of either of his two pursuers or the bomber he had nearly collided with and he could only assume that turbulence created by his sudden climb had caused the lighter Japanese fighters to go momentarily out of control and into the oncoming bomber. Stone's P-47N took him home across 300 miles of ocean to Ie Shima despite the lack of power. Confirmation of the burnt wreckage of aircraft later came from a reconnaissance photograph taken of the Japanese airfield. On this day, the 318th FG brought its claims for enemy aircraft destroyed while operating from Ie Shima to 102. Considerable numbers of Japanese aircraft had been encountered on nearly every mission since the middle of May.

Two other P-47N equipped groups joined the 318th on Ie Shima in May and June 1945. These were part of a force of very long range escort fighters activated in the US during October 1944 with the express purpose of providing escort for B-29 Superfortresses on their strikes against Japan. Four of these groups were trained on the older model Thunderbolts prior to receiving P-47Ns. A change of plan saw one group, the 508th, transferred to Hawaii in January to take over from another fighter group that had shed its P-47Ds for P-51s and been ordered to the Marianas. The 508th

Right Dee-Icer, a D-11-RE of 73rd FS about to be catapulted from the deck of the *USS Manilla Bay*. Cables attached to undercarriage automatically released at end of run.

Middle 73rd FS's 42-75379, alias *Head-up N'Locked*, which was set alight by a Japanese soldier on 26 June 1944.

Below Ground crew cleaning a P-47D-30-RE assigned to the Mexican 201st Squadron at Mindoro airfield, Philippines, August 1945. The US insignia is still retained under the right wing of this aircraft.

Left Major Harry McAfee (left) inspects the first of his squadron's aircraft hit by Japanese ground fire on Saipan. The 19th FS removed the camouflage paint from the tails and cowls of their P-47s as a distinctive marking. *Middle* Major McAfee about to taxi out in his personal P-47D-20-RA (43-25429). Two M65 1,000 lb bombs are suspended from the wing pylons. *Below* P-47Ns of 73rd FS taxiing along the airfield perimeter on rocky Ie Shima.

Right Distinctive heart marking used as insignia on some 21st FS P-47Ns. (E. D. Schlueter) *Middle* Yellow tail surface with blue triangles marked 463rd FS P-47Ns.° Photo taken at 30,000 ft an altitude where the heavy fighter achieved its best performance. (R. T. Forrest) *Below* Filling 165 gallon capacity tanks of 318th FG Ns prior to a mission. Total fuel carried on such occasions was 686 US gallons. Extra large 300 gallon drop tanks were available for further increasing the fuel load but were considered too unwieldy and were rarely used.

Left A Fifth Air Force P-47D-30-RA (with dorsal fin) landing at Naha, Okinawa in September 1945. Black bands round fuselage and wings were type identity markings. (R. Hegge) *Middle* Japanese anti-aircraft fire blasted a hole through the wing and tore away a large area of skin on this 318th FG P-47N leaving the underside of ammunition trays exposed. Note coloured downward recognition lights. Pilot is 1/Lt John Dooling. *Bottom* Servicing recently arrived P-47Ns of 464th FS, 507th FG, on Ie Shima. Many of these aircraft were P-47N-1-REs incorporating field modifications and redesignated N-2-RE. P-47N armament was the same as earlier models but while the total number of rounds per gun could be increased to 500, a total of 267 rpg was recommended as normal. *Opposite top left* Mechanics at work under the hot Iwo Jima sun on a presentation aircraft. The city of Freedonia, Ohio raised the $80,000 price of a Thunderbolt in War Bonds and had this P-47N-5-RE named to mark its contribution. The fighter was personal mount of Major Lewis C. Murdock, Ops Officer, 413th FS. (Via Urban Drew) *Opposite top right* Detail of 'zero rail' rocket installation which made the P-47N a formidable ground attack aircraft. Bomb is 1,000 lb M65 type. (Republic) *Opposite middle* Parking area for 58th FG at Mindoro, Philippines. There was no need for aircraft dispersal in August 1945 when the threat of Japanese air attack was past. Horizontal band on cowling was the group identity marking. (AFM) *Opposite bottom* P-47Ns of 437th FS lined up on Iwo Jima after the end of hostilities. Black and yellow checkerboard markings are incomplete on some aircraft. The outboard guns have been removed to reduce wing loading and improve handling. (Via Al Anderson)

REPUBLIC P-47 THUNDERBOLT

thereafter functioned largely as a replacement training unit and ferried both P-47s and P-51s to the combat units further west.

The other groups started to receive P-47Ns from late January onwards and by early April the first to complete training, the 413th, was on its way to Ie Shima. Although a new group, the 413th had two famous squadrons assigned, the 21st and 34th, that had borne the brunt of the air fighting in Java early in 1942. The third squadron was the 1st Fighter. The 507th Group arrived in Ie Shima in June to bring the number of P-47Ns on the island to over 250. Last P-47N group sent out, the 414th, went to the newly-acquired island of Iwo Jima which lay about half way between the B-29 bases in the Marianas and Japan and some 900 miles from the other P-47 groups on Ie Shima.

The excellence of the P-47 in ground attack saw the Thunderbolts assigned rarely to escort and often to harassing anything Japanese that moved on the surface of land or water. Railways, airfields and shipping came in for most attention and the three groups were regularly engaged in using the very telling firepower of their aircraft to create considerable havoc to the Japanese war economy. Only once did the three groups take part in an escort of B-29s on a daylight mission. On 8 August, 1945 some 400 B-29s flew to bomb Yawata, a major Japanese steel-producing city on Kyushu. A force of 151 P-47Ns met the bombers before the target and flying at a lower altitude kept watch for any enemy fighters climbing to intercept. They were not to be disappointed as the strongest force of interceptors – about 60 – ever encountered over Kyushu appeared and in a swift action 13 were claimed for the loss of five Thunderbolts. Four of the

US pilots bailed out over the sea. Contact with Japanese fighters was infrequent and the next sizeable battle occurred five days later when the 507th Group ran into a very large formation during a sweep over Korea. The enemy attempted interception but the scoreboard read, after a 30-minute engagement, one P-47N lost for claims of 20 Japanese aircraft destroyed.

The P-47N proved an extremely reliable combination of airframe and engine that gave pilots confidence on the long, over-water flights, It was undoubtedly more hardy than the nimble Mustang and had the war in the Pacific continued further fighter groups would have been redeployed to the Pacific and equipped with the type. The one real shortcoming was the long take-off run needed to get the fully loaded heavyweight airborne. The runways on Ie Shima and Iwo Jima were over $1\frac{1}{2}$ miles long yet pilots deemed it necessary to select high power settings to get their charges moving at very high speeds prior to lift-off. Failure had unpleasant prospects as the rocky surface of these islands was far from ideal for belly landings or run-overs, and beyond lay the sea. It was said that a visiting representative of the manufacturers considered too much fuel was being wasted on take-off through the selection of too high manifold boost. He explained that optimum settings had been worked out in the US for P-47s with full loads and to prove that these were quite sufficient he prepared to demonstrate. The Thunderbolt began its roll down the runway gathering speed far too slowly in the view of the onlookers. Eventually, the tail left the ground but still speed appeared insufficient. At the end of the runway the pilot attempted to lift the aircraft off but it had not attained flying speed and crashed into the rocks ahead with fatal outcome.

10 Mods and Odds

No fighter aircraft of World War 2 was introduced into service without some mechanical problem or deficiency arising. Then the art of aircraft design and manufacture was such that many weaknesses were only highlighted by extensive operational use, and where there had been only limited prototype testing before production models came off the line, the situation was even more pronounced. The Thunderbolt was in this category yet once the initial problems of tail flutter and ignition failure on high altitude boost had been rectified, the aircraft proved remarkably troublefree.

As described, Republic were continually working to advance the design but worthwhile changes were often long in appearing on aircraft reaching units in combat zones. The major obstacle was always the tooling up and other factors necessary to introduce even a seemingly minor innovation on the production line. In combat theatres – where delays could be crucial, units often took matters into their own hands and many modifications to be found on Thunderbolts, as with other types, were often exclusive to a theatre and sometimes a fighter group.

The desire to increase the P-47's endurance saw several practical developments in combat zones and the system of pressurising external 'drop tanks', using the exhaust from the aircraft's vacuum pump, was originally devised at a United Kingdom experimental establishment where some of the tanks were also manufactured. After the original four-point suspension 200 gal ferry tank had been discarded, Eighth Air Force P-47s used the two-point metal tear-drop shaped tanks originally produced for the P-39 Airacobra. These could be pressurised and were known as 75 gallon tanks although their actual capacity was about 84 US gal. In September 1943 British-based P-47s began to use locally made 108 US gal metal tanks and subsequently paper-plastic composition products of a similar capacity – also locally produced. Ground clearance was an obstacle to larger tanks although in Australia the Fifth Air Force had devised a broad bodied or 'flat' tank that could hold 200 gallons. This had a four-point suspension and when new P-47s arrived in Australia with two-point shackles under the belly a 110 gal tank was fashioned locally. The availability of wing pylons, early in 1944, to enable a tank to be carried under each wing, was a great step forward in the endurance problem. In Britain P-47s were then chiefly making use of locally made 108 gal tanks or the US made 165 gal 'flat' tank. Mediterranean-based P-47s received 75 and a new 110 gal metal tank from US production while in New Guinea the Fifth Air Force preferred to use the P-38 150 gal tank developed for the P-38. This was an elongated tear-drop shape, later modified and called the 165 gal tank to add confusion to the scene. However, this article became the standard P-47 tank during the latter stages of the Pacific War. A problem arose: when released the tank tumbled and the rear sometimes struck and damaged the ailerons or flaps. To overcome this some P-47 units wired the fins from a 1,000 lb bomb onto the rear of the tank so that the tank assumed a bomb trajectory when released.

Colossal 300 US gal tanks of similar shape to the 165s were also available in the Pacific although rarely used. One occasion was a long-range support mission flown by the 35th Group from Morotai, an island west of New Guinea, to Balikpapan in Borneo, a distance of 840 miles. The Thunderbolts involved carried a 300 gallon unit, partially filled, under one wing and a 165 under the other, posing precarious take-off problems, but successfully accomplished. The 'flat' 165 gal of US manufacture became the most commonly used tank on tactical Thunderbolts in Europe during the last year of the war. When the 56th Group received the P-47M, locally made 215 gal 'flat' tanks were used on the belly shackles so that the speed restricting wing pylons could be removed. By this date fuel could be conserved and range extended by shallow, low-power climbs to altitude as there was no longer the necessity to cross the continental coastline at a flak minimising high altitude.

Cruise control became a fine art in the SWPA where fighters had often to fly long distances to reach their objectives, although usually over water where enemy action was unlikely to be encountered. By the end of 1943, Fifth Air Force Thunderbolts could, depending on condition and load, obtain an endurance of $5\frac{3}{4}$ to 6 hours with the P-47C and early P-47D at optimum altitude, and still have a safety margin of 70 to 90 gal when landing. To do this, speed was reduced to 150 mph indicated with power settings at 1600 rpm and 35-in Mercury boost with the external 200 gal belly tank in place, and at 1400 rpm and 32-in Mercury boost without the tank.

A problem with external tanks was knowing when fuel was expended. This and the attendent human shortcomings with the fuel switching on internal tanks led Materiel Command, Wright Field, to request one of its agencies to work on an automatic fuel transfer system. This embodied automatic switching from depleted tanks to full ones and overcame the risk of pilot's failure to do so manually, and the not infrequent problem of inaccurate fuel gauges. There were several known instances of pilots overlooking fuel tank changes when engaged in combat. Engine failure in such circumstances, particularly at low altitude, could have disastrous consequences. The installation and testing was carried out early in March 1944, using P-47B 41-6038, with conclusions that the system was of great value and should be installed in the Thunderbolt and other fighters. However, this was never adopted in production.

Few pilots were anything but impressed by the Thunderbolt's firepower and the 8-gun armament remained virtually unchanged on all production models. In some combat units two guns were removed to reduce weight and enhance manoeuvrability, while in others where contact with the enemy was remote, only two guns were carried in each wing. There was a project to fit an alternative armament of four 20 mm cannon which apparently never came to fruition, although the Eighth Air Force did produce an experimental 20 mm cannon package installation slung on the wing pylon. Intended to enhance the P-47's effectiveness in ground attack it proved unstable and, in the opinion of a testing pilot, likely to tear the wings off the aircraft when being fired.

The advent of the B-7 shackles on the underside of fuselage and wings led to all sorts of ordnance being hung on Thunderbolts. General Purpose 500 and 1,000 lb bombs and Fragmentation Clusters were the types most commonly used in combat, but towards the end of hostilities petroleum mixture incendiaries — napalm — in modified drop tanks, were often carried. Early improvised incendiaries used by some units con-

sisted of small incendiary bombs strapped to an oil-filled drop tank. A special smoke maker unit also became available in 1945 for fitting to wing pylon shackles with the object of providing friendly ground forces with concealment.

Rocket projectiles had been successfully developed for air-to-ground launching in Europe and during 1942 the Army Air Forces' Ordnance Department began experiments using the infantry rocket and steel tube launchers. Though trials were reasonably successful the weight of these assemblies was undesirably high. The weapons were intended for most current US fighter types but due to its excellent stability and strength the P-47 became the favoured vehicle. The British had devised less bulky equipment for installing rocket projectiles on their ground attack aircraft and in December 1943 Wright Field experimented with these railed launchers, fitting two under each wing of P-47D-5-RE, 42-8053. RAF personnel supervised the work and a British test pilot made a satisfactory report after flying the aircraft to determine if the installation affected handling characteristics.

Meanwhile, special lightweight launch tubes had been developed for the original 'Bazooka'-like weapons and as this also presented much simpler initial installation it became the preferred type eventually put into production. The launch tubes were made from an inflammable plastic-paper composition with quarter-inch thick walls and two three-tube clusters loaded with projectiles weighed only 450 lb. Tubes were aligned with the wing guns so that the normal cockpit sight could be used to aim both weapons. While the rocket projectile was a very effective weapon against armoured vehicles it proved difficult to launch accurately and was frequently unreliable. The launch tubes were considered unwieldy and few pilots were happy with these appendages on their aircraft. The aerodynamic objections to the tube launchers and development work in the United States eventually produced a system requiring neither rails nor guides, 5-inch, high velocity rockets being attached to small pylons fitted to the undersurface of the wing. A total of ten rockets could be carried and factory installation commenced with the P-47D-30-RE.

Two gunsights were fitted to the majority of P-47C and D models, one being the Mk VIII reflector sight and the other a back-up, a simple ring and post. One Ninth Air Force group, the 406th, replaced the original 70-mm sight with a British 100-mm sight which was easier to use. Before the K-14 gyroscopic gunsight was factory-installed late in 1944, many P-47s serving in

Right P-47D-30-REs and Thunderbolt Mk IIs awaiting delivery at Farmingdale, summer 1944. Overseas shipments all passed through theatre modification centres before reaching combat units. (Republic)

Right UK-fabricated 215 gallon drop tank; a crudely welded but effective steel unit. Mechanic's jacket is draped over top. *Below* To prevent released drop tanks striking the wing and damaging flaps, a spring loaded fork arm pressed against the rear of the tank. The arm snapped up against the pylon when the tank fell clear. Fuel line was severed by means of an easily broken glass elbow. Demonstration release on a 50th FG P-47D

Above M10 4.5-inch rocket projectiles used in tube cluster. Warhead is part painted yellow. (Republic)

Left Experimental 20 mm cannon installation attached to wing pylon shackle of 78th FG P-47D. *Opposite bottom* Bubble panel on canopy of 365th FG P-47D.
Right Malcolm Hood installed on a P-47D-4-RA used for training in England. (Via Merle Olmsted) *Middle top* A special ski undercarriage tried out on a P-47G by Wright Field in 1944. (AFM)
Middle bottom Many 'war-weary' P-47s were modified to carry a passenger by removal of equipment directly behind the pilot's seat. Col Ray Stecker, CO of 365th FG, prepares to take his Crew Chief, S/Sgt Bailey Ingram, for a flight.
Below left Bubble panel which allowed pilot to glance back over tail. (E. Meindle)
Below right Camera installation in a specially fashioned wing pylon fairing on Col George Lee's P-47D. Lee was CO of 86th FG in final months of the war and completed his 250th combat sortie on 26 March 1945 – a record for a tactical pilot in the ETO.

Left Red-nosed 56th FG P-47M with M-10 smoke tanks fitted on the wing pylons. These were intended for laying defensive smoke screens at low altitude. (Russell Zorn) *Below* British rocket equipment on P-47D 42-8053 at Wright Field. (AFM)

Left Post-war installation of bomb fins on 165 gallon drop tanks. Aircraft is a P-47N. (AFM)

Europe had been base- or depot-modified to receive this sight. The K-14 gave great advantages in accurate shooting, particularly with deflection shots.

The original high spine fuselage (the term 'razor-back' to distinguish this configuration did not come into popular use until well after World War 2) restricted vision aft. The production rear view mirror, mounted above the windshield framing, was generally considered inadequate for letting a pilot see if he was being pursued. Various mirror arrangements were so sported by Thunderbolts in combat squadrons, usually as the pilot desired on his assigned aircraft. Three mirrors were not uncommon, the two additional items being fixed one each side to the fuselage below the windshield framing. A few P-47s in Europe dispensed with the original fitment and had two large Spitfire-type mirrors fixed to the top of the windshield framing. Another method of improving the outlook from the cockpit was the use of plexiglass 'bubble' panels. Originally supplied for installation in B-26 and other bomber observation windows, the side plexiglass of the P-47's canopy was removed and the bubble panel fitted in place, enabling a pilot to look back at his own aircraft's tail. The 'blown' perspex canopy, known as the Malcolm Hood, that the British used on Mustangs was also adapted for the Thunderbolt and although highly popular was always in short supply.

In Europe, where engineering facilities were good, significant modifications were usually carried out at depots and, for the sake of conformity, individual units were not encouraged to make unauthorised changes. In the Pacific where air depots could not depend on local engineering back-up, individual units did foster particular refinements to a much larger degree. An example of this is the changes made to Thunderbolts of the 35th Group in the SWPA. A small mast was installed on the fin to raise the radio antennae about one foot to improve reception and range. The Mk VIII gunsight was raised 2 inches by means of a bracket, to give better vision for deflection shots. A door was cut in the rear fuselage for easier access to the inter-cooler motor. An on-off switch was linked to the water-injection pressure pump so that it could be shut off and not be left to run continuously. The arrangement of 'stick' controls was changed so the bomb release trigger was on top of the stick and a microphone button just below the hand grip. Three electrical toggle switches were installed in the cockpit so that a pilot could select the dropping of either or both wing stores, armed or safe. Other P-47 groups in the war with Japan had their preferred modifications, some similar, some different to the 35th's.

11 End of the Line

Production of the Thunderbolt was terminated in the autumn of 1945 with the cancellation of contracts for nearly 6,000 P-47Ns. Evansville delivered its final aircraft in September and the Farmingdale lines stopped in October, although a few aircraft were not actually turned over to the USAAF until the end of the year.

When hostilities ceased in Europe there were over 3,000 Thunderbolts at stations in Germany, France, Italy and the United Kingdom. Many were brand new replacements with only a few hours on them and these were flown to Speke near Liverpool, England, to be disassembled and prepared for shipment to the USA and the Pacific theatre. Among the first to go were five P-47N-5-REs, which allegedly had been destined for the 56th Group but got no further than a modification depot before the war ended. The majority, however, were P-47D-30 and 40-RAs earmarked for the tactical air forces on the continent. Many aircraft in squadron service were later moved to Speke and sent home but a vast number were never to leave Europe. Several of the original P-47Cs, the first P-47s in action, were still flying in Europe for training purposes and these were broken up for scrap. In Germany where the great majority of Thunderbolts finished up, several airfields, including Kassel, became collection stations where row upon row of Thunderbolts stood waiting for the breaker's bar, their many different markings making a colourful picture.

Some Thunderbolts went to a replacement pool for the six P-47D equipped fighter groups that remained in Germany as part of the occupational forces. Drawn from the Ninth and Twelfth Air Forces, these were the 36th, 79th, 86th, 366th, 368th and 406th Groups. They did not, however, endure long. By February 1946, the 36th and 86th were so depleted of personnel that they were wound up. In August the same year changes of designation took place and the 366th, 368th and 406th became the 27th, 78th and 86th respectively. By the following June all but the 86th Group had ceased to exist in Germany and the last P-47s operated by the USAAF in Europe were with this unit at Nordholz.

At the time of Japan's surrender about 1,400 Thunderbolts both first and second line were with units engaged in that war, just over a thousand being with the air forces on the island chains surrounding Japan. As in Europe, some aircraft were scrapped, others sent home or were stored, or remained serving with the occupational groups, the 58th and 413th. The 414th Group also remained active for some months, moving to the Philippines. Like their European counterparts, the occupation groups did not endure long being inactivated during 1946.

There was another way of disposing of surplus military aircraft, selling them to nations with no aircraft industry of their own – or one unable to provide modern military designs. In the immediate post-war years several nations availed themselves of the comparatively bargain rate offers of US warplanes and the Thunderbolt was a popular choice. The Republic of China formed its 11th Fighter Group into a P-47D equipped unit, using many of the aircraft from the USAAF's inactivated units in the western Pacific and south-east Asia areas. From Europe Thunderbolts were sold to Italy, Turkey, Iran, Portugal and Yugoslavia, while France whose units with the 1st Tactical Air Force had been flying P-47Ds received 131 shortly after VE day. These were used by *3ᵉ* and *4ᵉ* *Escadres de Chasse*, with an establishment of 32 aircraft each. The largest interest in Thunderbolts was shown by the central and south American nations, Bolivia, Chile, Colombia, Dominica, Ecuador, Honduras, Nicaragua and Venezuela, all acquiring P-47s during the decade following the war while Mexico and Brazil retained the type in their air forces. Many of these remained in service through two decades. The last were probably those few remaining with the Peruvian Air Force which were retired in 1969. The Thunderbolt's guns were not stilled for long after World War 2 and in addition to the RAF's operations over Indonesia, the French in Algeria and the Nationalist Chinese also used them in anger. Possibly the last offensive sorties were flown during the Dominican troubles of 1964.

Above P-47N-20-RE operated by negro-manned 332nd FG during early post-war years. *Right* One of the aircraft assigned to EEC 3/10, a pre-operational unit, at Dijon-Longvic in the early 1950s. The unit later moved to North Africa under another designation. (B. Regnier) *Below right* The French operated P-47s in Europe and North Africa until as late as 1960. Still sporting a WW 2 war record of 75 sorties, 44-89788 seen on a visit to Tempelhof, Berlin, 1948. (Via Dave Birch) *Below* Several P-47s were supplied to the Chinese Nationalists on Formosa during the 1950s. These P-47Ns were photographed at Toa-Yuan airfield on 14 February, 1955.

Left Many Air National Guard squadrons used Thunderbolts during the decade following World War 2. Here part-timers of 146th FS, Pennsylvania, prepare to despatch one of their aircraft. Battery booster trolley has line into engine compartment. One mechanic stands near fire extinguisher in case of a back-fire. (Via David Menard) *Middle top* Republic's rejuvenated P-47D, 42-23278, landing at Biggin Hill, England in 1963. A D/F aerial was fitted to the underside of the fuselage. (Republic) *Middle bottom left* Glenn Bach, the Republic test pilot who flew the Thunderbolt in Europe during 1963. Nose insignia combines national flags of nations that used Thunderbolts during World War 2. (Republic)

Above The P-47G owned by Ontario Air Museum, California in the 1970s and painted in the colours of the old 78th FG, Eighth Air Force. (A. Pearcy) *Left* The Brazilian Thunderbolt destroyed by student riots in 1969. (J. M. Davis)

Right Gate Guardian. Display P-47N at Perrin AFB, Texas in 1969. The aircraft formerly flew with Puerto Rico ANG. (Norman Taylor) *Middle top* Post-war updating of equipment often saw new block numbers given and this P-47N of the 199th FS, Hawaiian ANG, originally a 5-RE became 7-RE. (David Menard) *Middle bottom* National Air Museum's P-47D-30-RA loaned for Republic's Thunderbolt 20th anniversary celebrations on 2 May 1961. The 2 May 1941 was date given for XP-47B's completion and 6 May as day of first flight. *Below right* One of 50 P-47Ds turned over to the Italian Air Force by the USAF in 1950. 44-9008 had previously served with the 86th FG in Germany. (AFM) *Below left* A special Curtiss Wright propeller with supersonic blades on a P-47D at Caldwell, N.J. The aircraft was used in high speed dives to test the characteristics of these blades. (AFM)

REPUBLIC P-47 THUNDERBOLT

In the United States P-47s remained with a few regular air force fighter groups during 1946 and 1947, chiefly the re-organised 56th at Selfridge Field, Michigan and the 14th at Dow Field, Maine. The jet age had arrived and by the end of 1948 few active P-47s remained on the inventory of the regular Air Force. The reserve, notably the Air National Guard (ANG) a state territorial organisation, made use of the Thunderbolt in the eastern states. By 1950, it had 500 on hand of which 350 were in commission. The P-47 survived with the ANG until 1952 when jet aircraft released by the USAAF were available to take their place.

The revived Bendix Air Races in 1946 saw one Thunderbolt contestant, the first YP-47M stripped of all military equipment and entered by Bill Odom. This fastest of the conventional Thunderbolt models had good possibilities in competition with Mustangs and Corsairs but it seemed dogged with minor fuel troubles which prevented it from achieving any notable success. This particular aircraft later found its way to an aircraft dealer's yard in Oklahoma where it was cannibalised for parts for many years.

Of the 6,500-odd Thunderbolts that existed at the end of World War 2, few remained by the early 1960s and in consequence what had been looked upon as war surplus and potential scrap gradually became an historic relic. Republic themselves were one of the first to draw attention to the scarcity of their once plentiful product. They decided to mark the 20th anniversary of the first flight of XP-47 with a reunion to which any former Thunderbolt pilot was invited to attend. Republic then looked round for a flyable example of the P-47, eventually locating a D model held by Bob Bean, an aircraft dealer in California. This aircraft was flown back to Farmingdale and put through its paces before the 873 'Jug' pilots who turned up for the 2 May 1961 reunion.

The nickname 'Jug' was a shortened form of 'Juggernaut', a sobriquet for the P-47 dreamed up by sceptical pilots in the days when the aircraft looked anything but a fighter. Only after hostilities did 'Jug' grow in popularity as a familiar term for the P-47, wartime pilots usually referring to the aircraft by its true names or by the shortened 'T-bolt'.

Republic's P-47D was repainted with camouflage and markings similar to those carried by the wartime P-47D of ace Robert Johnson. The aircraft was in such good condition that it was decided to exhibit it at the 1963 Paris Salon, then the most influential aircraft manufacturers' show in the world. The P-47 was dismantled into major components, crated and shipped to St. Nazaire. On re-assembly it was flown not only at Paris but other air displays in France, Germany, Belgium and the UK. Its pilot Glenn Bach, Republic's chief production test pilot on jets, was no stranger to the Thunderbolt having flown one operationally with the 359th Fighter Group from East Wretham in the UK during the winter of 1943-44. Maintenance was in the hands of T. Maclaughlin, a Republic engineer who had worked at Farmingdale on P-47 maintenance problems during the production years.

After its demonstration flights in Europe the Thunderbolt was returned to Republic, overhauled and flown at displays in the USA. In 1965 Republic donated the aircraft to the Air Force Museum, Dayton, Ohio, where it was put on permanent static exhibition. Two other static Thunderbolts, both N models, were parked outside the gates of Peterson AFB, Colorado, and Lackland AFB, Texas, during the late sixties. The Smithsonian has a P-47D-30-RE, while the Ontario Air Museum, California, has a G model once painted up in the colours of 56th ace Walker Mahurin's personal 'mount'. The YP-47M racer resides in the private air museum of Earl Reinert at Wheeling, Illinois, but in an incomplete state. The other Thunderbolts known preserved in the USA include seven ex-Peruvian Air Force P-47Ds which were acquired by the self-styled Confederate Air Force at Harlingen, Texas. Some of these aircraft are regularly flown on a club basis.

Abroad a lone P-47D resides in the Turkish Air Force Museum, and the French have preserved an example at Paris. The Brazilians erected one of their examples on a plinth in a Rio park. Left-wing students apparently objected to this American warplane, dormant as it was, and during riots in that city during 1969 the Thunderbolt was brought down in flames.

There are other physical remnants of the 15,683 Thunderbolts made between May 1941 and December 1945. A few are buried deep under English meadows. Some encrusted fragments still lie in the ocean bed, while other crumbling wrecks are overgrown in the rain soaked forests of New Guinea. The residue of the multitude still exists. But for most men who knew it the Thunderbolt is a memory — an exhilarating memory of a wondrous military monster on the ground that, once having gained its true element far above the earth, became transformed into a fulminating missile, indeed, the very manifestation of its name — a thunderbolt.

12 Pilot Opinion

The characteristics of the various Thunderbolt models have been discussed in the narrative on this aircraft's development and service use. However, an overall assessment of the fighter is best obtained from the detailed observations of service pilots who flew it in combat. The following accounts have been selected from experienced pilots of different nationalities and service backgrounds who flew Thunderbolts in contrasting roles in widely separated war zones. Significantly their comments are broadly in agreement on many aspects, underlining the principal advantages and disadvantages of this aircraft.

EUROPE: WITOLD LANOWSKI

'When I was flying Spitfires in the Polish Air Force in 1943 we occasionally met Thunderbolts and had friendly "fights". This was at low altitudes and we could out-climb and out-turn them – it was easy to get on their tails. We laughed about them and said, "This is not a fighter, it is a flying barrel!" At the time I would not have been very happy if someone had told me I would one day be flying a Thunderbolt on operations. That such a big aircraft could be considered a fighter was silly in my opinion.

'In autumn 1943 I was assigned to a desk job – to my disgust. By then I had completed 97 operational flights. There were many other experienced Polish pilots being similarly placed and many of us had no intention of being grounded if we could possibly help it. The question was resolved when the Americans invited some of us to fly with them and eventually permission was obtained from Air Ministry for six of us to go on short-term loan to the 56th Fighter Group. It was a reciprocal gesture of friendship that had begun in 1919 when American fighter pilots (the originators of the first Kosciuszko Fighter Squadron) flew in Poland in her defence against the Bolsheviks; and later, in 1941 and 1942 American Poles trained and flew in the Polish Air Force under British Command. Francis Gabreski was one of these American Polish pilots and later as a USAAF Lieutenant Colonel commanded the 61st Fighter Squadron in the 56th Group. So in May 1944 we went to Boxted and formed a Polish flight in Gabreski's squadron. I was going to fly the Thunderbolt! But Thunderbolt or whatever, at least I was going to fight.

'My immediate reaction was amazement at the size of this single-seater. Climbing up the enormous fuselage and getting into the wide cockpit, it was hard to believe I was in a fighter. It was just like sitting in an armchair, I had space everywhere, fantastic visibility. (The pilot fitted like a hand in a glove in the other fighters I had flown – in the French Caudron C714 the perspex was a half-inch from my shoulders and there was hardly room to turn my head.) At the same time there was a satisfaction in being in such a large, powerful machine. I had laughed at it once but the Americans had shown what it could do; and in no time at all she gained my complete respect and admiration.

'There wasn't any time for a conversion course. Everyone on the aerodrome was too busy. They said here is the aircraft, explained what is what, and off I went. All six of us were experienced and had flown many types of aircraft, so the Thunderbolt was one more and was no problem to fly once you knew where everything was in the cockpit. The Spitfire was relatively simple; the amount of clocks and gauges you had were negligible; the supercharger was automatic and from a simplicity angle piloting was easy. In comparison, the Thunderbolt was complicated, but in many ways easier to fly. When you took-off or landed the Thunderbolt never really swung and you could lock the tail wheel to keep it straight down the runway. The undercarriage was set very wide and, really, you had to be a bloody awful pilot to have an accident in a Thunderbolt – if there was nothing mechanically wrong. With the Spitfire with its narrow track undercarriage take-off and landing required a lot more skill, especially in winter in snow and on the it could be held on a steady course. Another thing that was good was the cockpit heating. We didn't have this in the Spitfire which made it more difficult to be efficient if you were half frozen.

'The biggest disadvantage of the Thunderbolt was

its weight and we knew we would have to fight in a different way to that in Spitfires. On the other hand it possessed the capacity to give an extra 400 hp by means of water injection, for use in an emergency, but only for a few minutes otherwise you blew your engine to pieces. I don't think there was any aircraft at the time that would dive so fast as a Thunderbolt. First time I dived after an enemy plane I came up with him so quickly it was a bit of a shock. The Germans nearly always dived to escape; just flip over and down. So we could easily catch them with the superior speed of the Thunderbolt – but it gained so quickly I am sure there must have been some collisions. Later models even had dive brakes. The Thunderbolt would turn quite well at speed but it was not safe to try and turn too far with a 190 or 109. It was best to go only half circle, shoot and then pull out; or three-quarters of a circle at the most. I had several engagements with German fighters at heights of between 5,000 and 10,000 ft. Dogfighting with them in a Thunderbolt needed care, it was not for the inexperienced. It was better to clear your tail, make a swift attack, then dive away. The only Thunderbolt pilot I saw hit and go down in a dogfight didn't check his tail. I shot the German off him but it was already too late. I considered the 190 a better aircraft than the Messerschmitt; it could give you a tougher fight. The problem was that in a mix-up you sometimes had difficulty at long range telling which was a P-47 and which was an Fw 190 as they both had radial engines. In fact, I once mistakenly fired on another Thunderbolt. Luckily I didn't hit him.

'The most impressive thing about the Thunderbolt for me was the armament. There was no time for gunnery practices when I joined the 56th so I had no experience of what the heavy Browning machine guns would do in combat. The first time I got on the tail of a Focke-Wulf and gave him a very short burst he absolutely exploded! It was fantastic! Nothing like this had ever happened in Spitfires due to the wide setting of the cannons (2) and machine guns (4), and small amount of rounds per cannon. Sometimes the enemy fighter would smoke but I had never seen one explode. The concentration and punch of bullets from those eight "Point-Fifties" in the Thunderbolt was tremendous. You could see where you were hitting which you rarely could with other fighters I flew. And if you saw where you were hitting all you had to do was pull your deflection, and there it was – explosion! I have always believed the principal reason the Thunderbolt did so well in air fighting was its firepower.

'I would say there was very little difference between the flight behaviour of the various Thunderbolt models

I flew. The bubble hood type gave a vast improvement in visibility and the hood, being electrically operated, was simple to ease open a few inches enabling you to get a breath of fresh air in the cockpit. Because the engine had a big appetite the cry was always for bigger tanks to carry more fuel. The first bubble hood P-47Ds were given to the leaders and we then had a problem because these aircraft had a bigger internal fuel tank. Some leaders would be busy chasing Germans and forget that they had more fuel than the other pilots.

'I never had any real mechanical problems on my Thunderbolt; the standard of American engineering was very good and our mechanics were excellent. Another good thing was that Republic had a permanent representative on the aerodrome who was constantly interested in what we wanted improved or modified. Because the 56th was such a successful group – and in my opinion a lot of this success was due to Hubert Zemke: he was the best leader of any nationality I served with – it often got new equipment to try out. We tested the rocket tubes fitted under the wings. Nobody liked them. There was a story that when some fellow fired his rockets they did a 180° turn and came back at him! We were one of the first to try napalm – I think it was Schilling who dropped some on the field at Boxted to see what would happen.

'Near the end of the war we got the very fast P-47M which we polished to get extra speed. It had the very good gyroscopic gunsight only I must admit that we were not really happy about the change as we had become so used to the old sight. Then there was the two-seat Thunderbolt which was fitted out with a radar set and had antenna sticking out from the wings. The idea was to try and find German aircraft in the air while we were over Germany. It wasn't successful as the radar did not function well and the aircraft was so much slower than the rest.

'The Thunderbolt was well known for the punishment it would take. I have seen one come back to Boxted with a top cylinder and piston blown completely off by a shell. No liquid-cooled engine fighter could take such punishment (I had a friend who was shot down in a Spitfire by a single rifle bullet in the cooling system – on manoeuvres in England!). Between 1935 and 1959 I flew more than forty different aircraft. The Thunderbolt wasn't the best propeller driven type I flew but during the war I never felt safer than I did in a Thunderbolt. It could take more and give more than any other single-seat fighter of its day.

'To make comparisons between the Thunderbolt and any other aircraft, such as the Spitfire, is not really justifiable in that its capacity and ability were totally different. Therefore it is somewhat unfair to make such comparisons. The Spitfire was a short range – per one battle, aircraft – Paris and back. The Thunderbolt was a long range (and with later models, a very long range) aircraft – 2 to 3, or even more, battles per mission – Berlin and back. Even so, this exceptional aircraft demanded greater experience plus additional training of its pilots to do it justice. But due to the progressive speed of the war itself and the demand so placed on the pilots, the US 8th Air Force had no option but to replace the Thunderbolts with the less demanding long range P-51 Mustang.

'However, the 56th Fighter Group, on their own request, were permitted to keep the Thunderbolt. As the top scoring American Group* (in air-to-air claims) it seemed fitting they should retain the remarkable Thunderbolt that had helped to make them one of the most famous fighter units of the war.'

*354th FG of Ninth AF had higher claims.

BURMA: JIM DOUBLE, RAF

'The overwhelming thing about coming to the Thunderbolt after Hurricanes was size; everything about it was bigger than on any single-engine type I had seen or flown. Any pilot who has flown a particular aircraft and become quite accustomed to its ways and confident in handling it, when he goes to the next one, no matter what it is, he always thinks he will never manage. Half the secret is becoming familiar with the cockpit; knowing automatically where everything is; doing it with blindfold checks. I sat in the Thunderbolt for hours to do this, and it took some time because there were an awful lot of dials and switches compared with the cockpit of a British fighter. When you drop in a Hurricane or Spitfire you seem to fit in the thing – the sides are nearly on you – you feel snug, more part of the aeroplane. By comparison the Thunderbolt cockpit was enormous and yet every corner seemed filled with levers and instruments. The joke among Thunderbolt pilots was that if you got into trouble in an air fight and had to take evasive action it was easier to undo your straps and run round the cockpit!

'I remember feeling lost in the thing when I taxied out for my first flight but there were so many things to do – lock tail wheel for take-off and carry out all those cockpit checks – that I never had time to feel apprehensive. I had been warned to sit back and put my head against the rest before undoing the taps. I soon learned the wisdom of this for when pushing the throttle full open there really was a lot of thrust,

whacking you in the back of the neck. As it hurtled down the runway I was aware that I had never been behind so much power, but grateful when this huge thing lifted off, I could flip the wheels up, and everything happened as it should. The climb-out was decidedly sluggish and the aircraft didn't impress in turns, but once you got the speed up it could be quite impressive in sharp manoeuvres. After a few trips I quickly forgot the concern of the first flight and it wasn't long before I was very happy to be flying Thunderbolts.

'I was part of the first intake at the new Thunderbolt OTU at Fayid, down on the Suez Canal. My instructor's report which stated "He is making good progress" has always been of some amusement as I'd probably flown the Thunderbolt more than he had. Some of the problems we were to come up against were no more known to the instructor than to the trainees. On my third trip in a Thunderbolt I was sent off to practise aerobatics. Playing safe I went to about twenty-eight thousand before putting it through the paces. Once you got the speed up it was quite a performer. Rolling off the top of a loop and accelerating down the Thunderbolt suddenly started shuddering. The stick simply flew out of my hand, the aircraft flipped over on its back and went straight down. I cut the throttle, centralised controls, the usual things to make a recovery, but as soon as I attempted to pull back on the stick there was this violent shuddering. Over on its back and down again, really unwinding fast. This happened three times and at about seven thousand I was seriously thinking of getting over the side. I had one more gentle go and to my relief it came out perfectly. Checked all controls but everything appeared all right. Gingerly came in to land – because I was very shaken by the whole episode. Just after I came in one of the so-called instructors arrived back equally white-faced and shaken, reporting just the same symptoms. So they stopped all flying, got in touch with the American technical people and posed our problem. The reply was "Compressibility". In the thin air I had obviously been doing all the wrong things, but compressibility was something none of us had come up against before. The Thunderbolt, being heavy and powerful built up very high speeds at high altitude and it wasn't until the lower, denser air slowed it up that recovery could be made.

'Early in 1945 I was posted East and after a three-week jungle survival course and a 30 hour flight refresher on "T-bolts" at Yelahanka, I joined No 79 Squadron. At the time the Squadron was based at Wangjing, near Imphal, with three other Thunderbolt

REPUBLIC P-47 THUNDERBOLT

squadrons all engaged in tactical ops, supporting the ground forces in driving the Japs out of Burma. We worked for the British Army and briefing and de-briefing was all done by their men. Seventy-nine was something of an international squadron, having two Americans, two South Africans, Canadians, a New Zealander, and an Indian, apart from the British boys. The CO "Gaddy" May was an Australian, a fantastic character who we all thought the world of. I had come out from England as a Warrant Officer with quite a lot of flying time and was probably the most experienced of the bunch of replacement pilots with whom I arrived. Apparently 79 was short of pilots and within about an hour of my arrival I had been loaned some flying kit and was on my first fighter patrol, flying No 2 to the CO — his policy with newcomers.

'The jungle strips from which we operated were very different from Fayid and its concrete runway. Some were just compacted soil and the all-weather strips had perforated steel plank runways which became covered with mud in the rainy season. They were of sufficient length for take off with a belly tank and two 500 lb bombs — the usual load — but there was little safety margin. Belly tanks were only used on the longer trips; most jobs could be managed on internal tanks. A Thunderbolt had a pretty rapid rate of descent with the power-off so our landing approaches were power-on, keeping at least 115 mph IAS (indicated air speed) with undercarriage lowered and part flap. If you had to land with stores under the wings then to play safe it had to be at least 120, which was quite fast to hit those slippery metal planks.

'Our average operation was between 2½ and 3 hours duration, and you would be drenched in sweat all the way. The cockpit was a hothouse. Sometimes the whole squadron (12 aircraft) would go, although often only 8 or 4 aircraft were required for a particular job. Most of the work was attacking enemy troops, supply dumps and communications, and there was some pretty intensive activity at times. The Japanese had their largest armies in Burma, their major land front in the war. When I first flew bombing strikes in Thunder-bolts the technique was to arrive over the target area at around 8,000 ft in echelon formation. Identification of the target would be confirmed by discussion over the radio. The leader would then roll over and dive straight down with the others following. Aim on the target was made with the reflector gunsight, screwing the aircraft around in the dive to keep on the spot. Bombs — which had instantaneous fusing — were released at between 1,500 and 1,000 ft just to give enough time to pull out. We would break out in different directions to avoid

running into each other. I only did a few of these vertical dive-bombing trips before tactics were changed. A few aircraft were seen to explode at the bottom of their dive; at first we thought they'd been hit by ground fire, then pilots began to report smelling petrol fumes in the cockpit. Investigation revealed that the main fuel tanks in some aircraft were leaking. The terrific G we were putting on the aircraft in pull-outs was causing fuel tanks to tear. From then on we carried 11-second delay bombs and made low diving attacks at an angle of about 30 degrees, keeping low after bomb release to make it more difficult for ground fire. We developed a habit of turning our heads after the appropriate delay to see our bombs explode. Once four of us were attacking a railway station and when I took a quick glance over my shoulder I saw two railway trucks in mid-air, the right way up, as if on some invisible rails in the sky.

'After bombing, the usual thing was to come round and strafe the target. We used all semi-armour piercing incendiaries as these would go through most of the protective reinforcing the Japs built up and also clear them out by starting fires. The firepower was terrific; you could literally demolish buildings with those eight guns. The only trouble we had was the blokes who kept their fingers on the trigger too long and burnt out gun barrels. All my operations were at low level and I never had to use oxygen. That is except unofficially after a hard night's drinking when a half hour in the cockpit for a "snifter" worked wonders clearing the head.

'The Thunderbolt was a hardy aircraft and gave us little trouble in the damp humid conditions that played the devil with some types. The only spot of bother I had was when I set off on an operation that was to be the last for my aircraft before it was sent back to a depot for overhaul. It was a whole squadron job; I did my ground check and pushed off when my turn came. All was fine until halfway down the runway, tail up and just about to come unstuck, when the engine started to miss. Bombed up, there was no way I could cut my run and stop without ending up in the trees off the end of the strip. The only thing was to push it through the gate for emergency power. The aircraft just came off stickily and I managed to get the undercart up as it scraped over the treetops. There was a village ahead but the bombs had to be jettisoned if the aircraft was to be kept in the air. The engine would pick up and then die, pick up again and falter once more, at times it barely kept me out of the trees. I began a gentle turn, crossed a Spitfire strip to the north of ours and sent everyone scattering as the Thunderbolt started to misfire and sink again. Somehow the engine produced

Right Witold 'Lanny' Lanowski in the cockpit of his P-47M-1-RE at Boxted. *Below left* Personal insignia on Lanowski's 44-21108 — the first production P-47M. *Below right* Cpt Drew's P-47N-5-RE, *Detroit Miss II*, *Bottom right* Urban 'Ben' Drew — complete with long-mission chin stubble! He was an ETO fighter ace before flying P-47Ns. *Bottom left* W/O James Double in the cockpit of NV:M, his usual Thunderbolt Mk II.

enough power to keep me flying and while the CO kept telling me over the radio to put down, there just wasn't a clear place. As luck had it my wide turn brought me back dead in line with our runway. Dropping the wheels I was able to set her down safely; there was somebody in there with me that day. Obviously a form of fuel starvation although they never did discover any mechanical fault in that engine.

'Everyone was impressed by the punishment the "T-bolt" would take. Once, after strafing barges, the squadron was flying low between two hills when somebody called out a Jap road convoy. Everyone was trying to pull round to get in a shot and the bloke in front of me left it so late that he was right down on the side of the hill when he came to break away. I saw him go clean through a clump of trees and disappear from sight. I thought "That's him." Suddenly there he was, still flying. He climbed away and apart from complaining that his aircraft was running hot, seemed okay. When we got home we all went over to have a look. The airscope was literally full of wood. They pulled out branches as thick as your wrist. Not a dent on the prop'; nothing wrong with the plane. The pilot got his leg pulled about his method of collecting us firewood.

'Such incidents gave you great faith in the Thunderbolt. We became very fond of it and used to engage in a lot of good natured banter with US pilots who came in with supplies. They'd say, "You got some good ships there, you guys". We'd retort, "Yeah, and it takes us to fly 'em!" I did know one fellow who admitted being frightened of the "T-bolt" – in wartime you got people who shouldn't have been flying but pushed themselves to stick it out. We were coming back from a job in monsoon weather, terrible visibility and just above the jungle, really hanging on to each other, when suddenly out of the corner of my eye I saw a flash but daren't look round. When we got back we found it was this bloke; he had hit a tree. Really tragic, particularly as it was one of our last jobs, when the A-bomb had been dropped and the Japs were giving up.

'There was a fitter and rigger assigned to look after each "T-bolt". Mine would work until midnight to keep it in shape, remove the mud and polish the surface. Great fellows. Must have broken their hearts if they saw those beautiful aircraft bulldozed at the end of the war.'

PACIFIC: URBAN DREW, USAAF

'First time I flew a Thunderbolt was during advanced fighter training at a Mustang base in Florida. We used P-47s to tow targets for air-to-air gunnery practice and thought of them strictly as tow-target ships. Compared to the P-51 it was something of an old truck. Admittedly the models we had were P-47Bs that had seen better days. And I never did get much experience of the total flexibility of their performance while towing a target around – my attention was more taken up with not getting shot down by one of the other students!

'After returning from my combat tour on P-51s in Europe, I was assigned to a pilot pool and headed for an instructional unit down on the Texas border. I didn't fancy instructing, particularly as the outfit had the slow AT-6 (Harvard/Texan), and I fretted to get back into combat. The only way was to gain the ear of somebody with influence, and hearing that my old P-51 group CO was not far away I called him for help. He left me in no doubt that there was no chance of getting back to Europe, but he did have a friend who was taking a P-47 group to the Pacific and might be able to use someone with my experience. With no other options I accepted his offer and soon received orders to proceed to Wilmington, North Carolina, where the P-47 outfit was based.

'I was to find that the group, the 414th, had already started to move to the Pacific theatre, as it turned out the last US fighter outfit to go to war. Only one P-47 remained on the base and that was the CO's – Colonel Thorne's. He asked me how long since I had flown a P-47 and when told of my experience in flying school said, "Well, this is a much later version and I think you'd better get at least a couple of hours on it. Only it's my airplane and I want it back here in the same condition as you find it now." So out I went, checked things over with the crew chief and studied the manual. Looked much the same as the earlier models. Took off and flew around for about thirty minutes and was just settling in when a couple of Marine Corsairs decided they'd like to mix it up a bit. It was soon obvious they could hold a tighter turn than I could and I decided the only way I was going to shake them was to bring in extra power by pushing the throttle full open. In about 30 seconds the engine started to bang and black smoke poured out. Too late I realised that it wasn't getting water-methanol and had over-heated. I had real difficulty in getting it back to base, which was around a hundred miles away, and once or twice thought I would have to bale out when the banging and coughing engine seemed it was going to quit. All I could think of was what the Colonel was going to say and whether I had just lost myself the trip to the Pacific. Sure enough when I taxied up to the ramp he was there; the noise from the engine and the black smoke it was throwing out told him all he wanted to know. Before I had time to get out of the cockpit he was up on the wing and with a few well chosen words reminded me of his caution. They had to change the engine but I was in part exonerated because the water-methanol tank was empty and there had been no indication of this on the Form 1 (aircraft status sheet handed to pilot by crew chief before a flight). Still, in the Colonel's opinion I had sinned by engaging in unauthorised manoeuvres and as a punishment I was sent on ahead of the rest of the Group pilots to help with getting the camp ready on Iwo Jima.

'This small island was about halfway between Japan and the Marianas where the B-29s were based. At 660 miles to the nearest point on Japan it was at extreme range for the P-47N and we wondered why we were based in Iwo and not on Ie Shima where the other three Thunderbolt groups were – only about 325 miles from Japan. As any time spent over Japan was going to be limited to about 15 to 20 minutes maximum it didn't make sense from a tactical standpoint. The rumour that we were on Iwo Jima ready to move in to Japan as soon as the invasion force acquired a strip seemed justified. As things happened we never found out as after only a few operations from Iwo in August 1945 the Japs quit.

'In flying the P-47N I was naturally going to use the Mustang as a yardstick for comparison. We had two P-51 groups on Iwo and the differences were the more sharply obvious to me when we tangled in mock dogfights. Above all I missed the responsiveness of the P-51: the P-47N was plain sluggish. I couldn't turn with Mustangs or carry out any manoeuvre without they had a head start. It was soon forcibly impressed on me that if my group was going to get into anything with the very tight turning Japanese fighters then we'd have to go back to the old bounce and zoom system that the P-47s had used quite effectively in Europe. Of course, the P-47N did have this tremendous dive capability and you could outdive a Mustang. Being a much heavier machine the P-47 needed more stick pressure. It rolled quite nicely, and would go through most manoeuvres without exhibiting any vices – once I flew it upside down for a fairly extended period. View from the cockpit was good in the P-47N and only forward over the big nose was visibility more restricted than with the P-51D. Surprisingly, the cockpit of the P-47 was quieter than the Mustang's – in my opinion – so I assume it was better insulated. The Thunderbolt was definitely more stable than the P-51, it didn't bounce around so much in rough air and as a gun platform it was superb. I much preferred it for ground strafing and those two extra 50-calibre guns seemed to make all the difference in chewing up a target. The wide-tread

undercarriage was another good point and I would say a novice pilot would have an easier time taking-off and landing than if in a Mustang. A Mustang always had a tendency to swing on take-off if you didn't lead rudder into it – violently if you applied power too quickly. The P-47N was much more stable on take-off – at least you were far less likely to get into trouble, and the same went for landing; it was an easy airplane to bring in despite the restricted view over the nose.

'That said, take-offs on operations were another matter because to make the round trip of more than 1,300 miles the airplane required full internal tanks, a 165 gallon (US) tank under each wing and 110 gallon tank under the belly for a total of over 900 gallons, giving a gross weight in excess of 10 tons. The runway at North Field, Iwo, was over a mile long but with a full load the P-47 accelerated so slowly you wondered every time whether you were going to make it – there was a drop off the cliff into the sea beyond the far end. It needed full power to get off and from then on everything was done to conserve fuel. A single orbit of the field was sufficient to get us into formation and then we would begin to climb out on course until we reached 20,000 ft for optimum fuel consumption. For safety, take-off was always made using the main tank. Then we would go over to the drop tanks for the sooner they could be drained and released the sooner we would be getting rid of some of the drag on the airplane. In the 15 to 20 minutes it took to climb to our operating altitude the P-47 would use all the fuel in the belly tank. Cruise would be at around 185 IAS and all the drop tank fuel would be gone by the time we reached Japan.

'Monotony was a problem, with nothing but ocean below for three or four hours at a stretch. The cockpit was roomy and you could shuffle about to relieve your bottom. Every pilot took drinking water in a large Thermos jug which we stood on the cockpit floor; you sure needed it. Being on oxygen for most of the time added to the discomfort. The P-47N had an automatic pilot, the first I'd ever seen in a fighter. The idea was to take away some of the fatigue on these long hauls. It tended to be unreliable and wasn't easy to set up. If you didn't get the co-ordinates set properly and turned the auto-pilot on the airplane would flip or dip. Most of us didn't bother with it and preferred to fly by hand. The Thunderbolt was easily trimmed out and then needed only light pressure on the stick in a level cruise.

'Our missions were mostly ground strafing airfields or some briefed military installation. The 414th never engaged any enemy fighters on these flights. What few aircraft the Japs did put up usually intercepted when you were starting the trip home, knowing that if they could keep you busy for a while you might not make it back to Iwo. Fact, finding the island was our biggest worry. We had a B-29 navigational 'plane lead us to Japan and it would orbit off the coast to lead us back, but you couldn't always find it. On Dead Reckoning alone there was plenty of room for error with 600 miles of ocean to cross. On my last mission my wingman was hit by ground fire while we were strafing. His P-47 was smoking as we climbed off target and he radioed that he might have to bale out. He managed to keep going for about 200 miles then the engine began to quit. In baling out he hit the tail, breaking both legs. I put out a distress call and circled over him for about 30 minutes until a B-29 arrived and dropped a raft. Then I set course for Iwo, only when it should have shown up it was nowhere to be seen. The gauges showed fuel for only a few minutes so I started calling "Mayday". I was more than relieved to pick up a very faint signal from Iwo giving me a vector – I was way out to the west and had to turn 90 degrees. You hear stories of guys who didn't have enough fuel left to taxi off the runway before the engine cut out; well in my case this is exactly what happened. Sad thing was that although the Navy picked up my wingman he must have had head injuries because he died when they got him to hospital. The few people we lost went down chiefly through running out of fuel. The P-47N was pretty reliable and I never had any malfunctions on mine. With the heavy loads and the heat we had a few tyre bursts. The engine was very dependable and I can say that I felt as safe as I've ever felt in combat when flying the Thunderbolt. Even so, have got to be honest and say that good airplane that it was, I would rather have been flying a Mustang.'

13 Engineering and Performance Data

Model and Block Number
Model designating letters were usually changed when: a new model engine was installed; a new model or type of propeller fitted; a major change in armament; or a major change in structure or equipment. In practice, this was not always the case and many such changes were only recognised by a new block number. Block numbers identify a group of aircraft incorporating the same modifications. These were supposedly to be assigned in multiples of five to production aircraft with intermediate numbers reserved for modifications made during service or at a modification centre. Again, this ruling was not adhered to in many instances.

Army Air Force Serials
The individual aircraft numbers assigned by the USAAF. Stamped on a data plate in the cockpit; applied in small black characters to the left side of fuselage in close proximity to the cockpit; and in abbreviated form on the fin. Note: Some P-47s laid down as one model were completed as prototypes of another.

Engine
Model installed at factory unless otherwise stated.

Propeller
As installed at factory. Changes occurred during service.

Dimensions
Dimensions varied slightly between individual aircraft of the same model. Data taken from Republic and USAAF documents. Height is for unladen aircraft on ground, measured from top of vertical propeller blade.

Weights
These also varied between individual aircraft of the same model and figures given are AAF standards. Gross figure is aircraft with pilot, normal fuel and war load but devoid of external stores. Maximum weight is the recommended limit for fully-loaded aircraft with external stores.

Speeds
Maximum speed is that obtained with aircraft clean of all external stores and pylons, and at gross weight. In most cases these speeds were obtained by water injection (War Emergency Power) and only sustained up to 15 minutes. All speeds varied with altitude and weight as well as between individual aircraft of the same model. The P-47 obtained its highest speeds around 30,000

Climb
Expressed in the time taken to reach a specified altitude from ground level. Times given are for the aircraft clean and at gross weight.

Service Ceiling
The point where rate of climb does not improve beyond 100 ft per minute. The practical limit for operational purposes.

Fuel
Internal, gives maximum built-in tankage. *External,* the maximum amount specified for drop tank loads. In both cases, the capacity is in US gallons.

Range
Maximum gives that obtained at retarded power setting on internal fuel stretching range to the limit. *Normal* is the usual distance obtained on internal fuel supplies at combat operating height and combat cruise speed. Range, however, varied enormously with weights, altitude and power settings.

Armament
Combat P-47s usually operated with all eight 0.50-in machine-guns installed. Ammunition was varied to meet the requirements of a particular mission. Figures given are those recommended by the AAF.

Changes
Changes made on the factory production line to bring about a new designation for a model. Changes at modification centres and at combat bases saw many of the older Thunderbolts up-dated. Instances exist where two aircraft from the same factory block, and serving on the same station, had different engines, propellers and other components. One aircraft had been extensively modified to meet a combat standard while the other had been restricted to training flights.

REPUBLIC P-47 THUNDERBOLT

Model	XP-47B
Quantity built	1
AAF Serial	40-3051
Engine	R-2800-17 & R-2800-35
Power rating	2,000 hp
Propeller	Curtiss Electric 12 ft 2 in dia
Dimensions: Span	40 ft $9\frac{5}{16}$ in
Length	35 ft $4\frac{3}{16}$ in*
Height	14 ft 2 in
Wing area	300 sq ft
Weights: Empty	9,189 lb
Gross	12,700 lb
Speeds: Max	412 mph at 25,800 ft
Landing	92 mph
Climb	5 min to 15,000 ft
Fuel: Internal	305 US gal
Range: Max	1,150 miles at 10,000 ft
Normal	575 miles at 25,000 ft
Armament:	Provision for 8 x 0.50 in machine-guns (mg) with 500 rounds per gun (rpg)

* Length increased by rudder changes.

General Description

Fuselage and components. Semi-monocoque, all-metal, stressed-skin construction, composed of transverse bulkheads and longitudinal stringers. Main, forward part of bulkhead/frame structure built in two units; top and bottom, bolted together. Aft section constructed as one complete unit and then assembled to forward sections. Front firewall bulkhead faced with stainless steel sheet. Engine attached by Lord mountings. NACA design type cowling formed by four quick-detachable panels fastened to support rings attached to engine valve rocker covers. Hydraulically operated cowling ventilation flaps fitted at rear of secondary engine cowling. Accessories, compartment aft engine with four cooling vents. Main fuel tank, 205 US gallons capacity situated forward and below cockpit between wing hinge bulkheads; 100 US gallon auxiliary tank directly aft rear wing hinge support bulkhead. 28 US gallon oil tank in accessory section. Oil cooling radiators with electrically operated outlet doors mounted in primary air duct beneath engine. General Electric exhaust-driven turbo-supercharger approximately 21 ft aft of propeller, in lower fuselage. Exhaust gases ducted to turbo through insulated pipes, one each side of lower fuselage. Exhaust gases released through waste gate (butterfly valve) housed in stainless steel hood under rear fuselage. Small waste gates at rear of engine for discharge of exhaust when not required for turbo power. Air for supercharging reaches turbo through long duct from lower engine cowl. After supercharging, air passes through intercooler prior to being piped back along either side of fuselage to single carburettor intake. Air for intercooling obtained from central duct and released on both sides of fuselage via electrically operated doors, which also affect temperature control.

Radio situated directly aft cockpit. Oxygen supply bottles mounted in upper compartment directly behind radio. Fully retracting tail wheel with enclosing doors. Access to cockpit via forward hinged door in left-side fuselage. Face-hardened armour plate $\frac{3}{8}$ in thick aft pilot's seat. Windshield of $1\frac{1}{2}$ in armoured glass.

Wings and associated components. Full cantilever type employing two main spars supporting attachment of wing to fuselage. Three secondary spars, one each supporting aileron, flap and undercarriage assemblies. Republic S-3 airfoil sections form multicellular structure with spars. Flush-riveted, stressed-skin surfaces reinforced by extruded angle stringers. Ailerons represent approximately 11.4% of total projected wing area. Fabric covered with push-pull rod system control. Controllable trim tab on left wing only. Landing flaps total 13% of projected wing area: NACA slotted trailing edge type, hydraulically-operated. Wing root chord of $109\frac{1}{2}$ in; mean aerodynamic chord of 87.46 in; 5.61 aspect ratio; angle of incidence +1°; top surface dihedral of 4 in; leading edge sweep-back 3°. Gun bays situated outboard of undercarriage well and actuating gear. Staggered arrangement for machine-guns allowing ammunition feed troughs to be arranged side by side in outer wing panels.

Empennage; Full cantilever structure. Total projected area: 81.45 sq ft. Fin and horizontal stabiliser cellular structure of flanged ribs secured to fore and aft spars in each plane. Whole unit bolted together and, in turn, bolted to rear fuselage brackets. Rudder and elevators originally fabric covered, later metal Handley Page type.

Remarks: XP-47B completed 2 May 1941. First flight 6 May 1941. Destroyed in crash 8 August 1942. Extensively modified during trials.

XP-47B, May 1941. According to Kartveli, the basic layout sketch of this fighter was drawn on the back of an envelope at a meeting at Wright Field in the spring of 1940. The olive drab fabric area of the rudder shows up clearly. (Republic)

P-47B, 41-5930 with fabric tail control surfaces, was used for test flying by the AAF at Patterson Field in the summer of 1942. Aircraft was destroyed in August 1943 when the pilot baled out after fuel fumes entered the cockpit. Note pilot sight lines to guns.

Model		P-47B
Quantity built		171
AAF Serials		41-5895 to 41-6065
Engine		R-2800-21
Power rating		2,000 hp
Propeller		Curtiss Electric C542S-A6 12 ft 2 in dia
Dimensions:	Span	40 ft 9 5/16 in
	Length	35 ft 4 3/16 in*
	Height	14 ft 2 in
	Wing area	300 sq ft
Weights:	Empty	9,346 lb
	Gross	12,245 lb
	Max	13,360 lb
Speeds:	Max	429 mph at 27,800 ft
	Landing	100 mph
	Climb	6.7 min to 15,000 ft
Service ceiling		42,000 ft
Fuel:	Internal	305 US gal
Range:	Max	835 miles at 10,000 ft
	Normal	550 miles at 25,000 ft
Armament:		6 or 8 x 0.50-in mg with 500 rpg

* Length altered by rudder changes.

Changes: General Electric A-13 turbo-supercharger regulator. Redesigned aerial mast for SCR-283 radio. Heightened pilot seat and cabin with sliding canopy (believed from 41-5896 onwards). New engine. Metal covered ailerons and trim surface changes. Windshield defroster introduced with 41-5951. With 41-5974 major changes in control surface movement limitations and tailplane incidence. The 34 x 9 mainwheel tyres increased from 8 to 10 ply rating from 41-5974. Modified link ejector chutes from guns on 41-6016 and subsequent aircraft.

Remarks: First P-47B completed December 1941 and accepted 21 December 1941. First of 4 pre-production aircraft completed 4 March. First 5 P-47B (41-5895 to 41-5899) considered pre-production test aircraft 1942. P-47B 41-6065 taken from line and completed as XP-47E. After completion, 41-5938 rebuilt as XP-47F. Designation of P-47B changed to RP-47B (Restricted) in 1944. Flight restrictions on all P-47Bs with fabric covered rudder and elevators. Most eventually modified to take metal covered tail surfaces.

Model		P-47C-RE	Speeds:	Max	429 mph
Quantity built		57		Landing	100 mph
AAF Serials		41-6067 to 41-6123		Climb	7 min to 15,000 ft
Engine		R-2800-21	Service ceiling		42,000 ft
Power rating		2,000 hp	Fuel:	Internal	305 US gal
Propeller		Curtiss Electric C542S 12 ft 2 in dia	Range:	Max	835 miles at 10,000 ft
				Normal	550 miles at 25,000 ft
Dimensions:	Span	40 ft 9 5/16 in	Armament:		6 or 8 x 0.50-in mg with 425 rpg
	Length	35 ft 5 3/16 in			
	Wing area	300 sq ft			
Weights:	Empty	9,350 lb			
	Gross	12,250 lb			
	Max	13,360 lb			

Changes: Strengthened and revised fin with metal covered rudder. Metal covered elevators. Additional oxygen and system revised – four D-2 cylinders (one in leading edge of

REPUBLIC P-47 THUNDERBOLT

left wing) in place of single F-1 cylinder in P-47B. A-17 turbo-supercharger regulator. Radio changes (SCR-274-N command set and SCR-515-A) with redesigned mast. Detail electrical changes. Minor changes were deletion of lower fuselage identification light and flap position indicator. New model gun camera and engine tachometer. Overall length increased by metal rudder.

Remarks: First aircraft completed 14 September 1942.

P-47C-RE. Increased oxygen supply for the pilot and revised tail surfaces to prevent failure in high-speed flight were notable improvements. *Betty* like other aircraft in the block, served with US based units. (AFM)

Model		P-47C-1-RE
Quantity built		55
AAF Serials		41-6066 & 41-6124 to 41-6177
Engine		R-2800-21
Power rating		2,000 hp
Propeller		Curtiss Electric C542S 12 ft 2 in dia
Dimensions:	Span	40 ft 9$\frac{5}{16}$ in
	Length	36 ft 1$\frac{3}{16}$ in
	Height	14 ft 3$\frac{5}{16}$ in
	Wing area	300 sq ft
Weights:	Empty	9,900 lb
	Gross	13,500 lb
	Max	14,925 lb
Speeds:	Max	420 mph at 30,000 ft
	Landing	104 mph
	Climb	7.2 min to 15,000 ft
		15 min to 25,000 ft
		20 min to 30,000 ft
Service ceiling		42,000 ft
Fuel:	Internal	305 US gal
	External	200 US gal
Range:	Max	835 miles at 10,000 ft
	Normal	400 miles at 25,000 ft
Armament:		6 or 8 x 0.50-in mg with 300 to 425 rpg

Changes: Fuselage extended by introduction of extra 8-in section forward of firewall giving improved flight characteristics through movement of the C of G. Alterations to layout of engine accessory section (only three vents in cover). Detail changes to main undercarriage and brakes. Tail wheel detail changes and elimination of steering. Revised supercharger air ducting. Electrical changes. Hydraulic flap equaliser.

Remarks: P-47C 41-6066 used as prototype for fuselage modification.

P-47C-1-RE had an extended nose section to improve C of G and allow more room in the engine accessories compartment. Fixed deflection plate between oil cooler shutter and exhaust waste gate was a feature distinguishing this model from previous Thunderbolts.

Model	P-47C-2-RE
Quantity built	128
AAF serials	41-6178 to 41-6305
Engine	R-2800-21
Power rating	2,000 hp
Other data similar to P-47C-1-RE	

Changes: Provision for four-point attachment of 200 gal ferry tank. Fuel and electrical changes.

P-47C-2-RE 41-6210, assigned to 62nd FS, was lost in combat with another unit in April 1944.

Model	P-47C-5-RE
Quantity built	362
AAF Serials	41-6306 to 41-6667
Engine	R-2800-21
Power rating	2,000 hp
Other data similar to P-47C-1-RE	

Changes: Radio, instruments and aerial. Cockpit heating.

P-47C-5-RE 41-6347
Lil' Abner (*right*), also
assigned to 62nd FS.
survived the war,
latterly as a non-
operational hack. This
aircraft was modified for
B-7 shackles and has
distinctive fuselage bulge.
(Republic)

Model	P-47D
Quantity built	4
AAF Serials	42-22250 to 42-22253
Engine	R-2800-21
Power rating	2,000 hp
Other data as late model P-47B	

Remarks: First Thunderbolts built at Evansville plant. Pre-production assembly during late summer and autumn on 1942.

P-47D. Last of the four pre-production Evansville Thunderbolts. (AFM)

Model	P-47D-RE
Quantity built	110
AAF Serials	42-22254 to 42-22363
Engine	R-2800-21
Power rating	2,000 hp
Other data similar to P-47C-2-RE	

Remarks: Originally only Evansville Thunderbolts were to be identified as P-47D and with the introduction of manufacturer identification letters the first Evansville block (line batch) became P-47D-RE. To aid product standardisation, following blocks from both plants were designated as P-47D, with Farmingdale continuing to use RE while Evansville adopted RA.

P-47D-RE. Most of the early Evansville production went to training units. Here USAAF personnel examine a D-RE in company with a P-51, P-40 and P-39.

Model	P-47D-1-RE		Height	14 ft 3$\frac{5}{16}$ in
Quality built	105		Wing area	300 sq ft
AAF Serials	42-7853 to 42-7957	Weights:	Empty	9,900 lb
Engine	R-2800-21		Gross	13,500 lb
Power rating	2,000 hp		Max	15,000 lb
Propeller	Curtiss Electric 12 ft 2 in dia	Speeds:	Max	420 mph at 30,000 ft
Dimensions: Span	40 ft 9$\frac{5}{16}$ in		Landing	104 mph
Length	36 ft 1$\frac{3}{16}$ in		Climb	7.2 min to 15,000 ft

REPUBLIC P-47 THUNDERBOLT

		11 min to 20,000 ft
		15 min to 25,000 ft
		20 min to 30,000 ft
Service ceiling		42,000 ft
Fuel:	Internal	305 US gal
	External	200 US gal
Range:	Max	835 miles at 10,000 ft (3.8 hrs)
	Normal	400 miles at 25,000 ft (1.3 hrs)
Armament:		6 x 0.50-in mg with 300 rpg or
		8 x 0.50-in mg with 425 rpg

Changes: Additional cowl flaps to improve cooling flow. Accessory compartment changes. Additional pilot armour in cockpit. Fuel system improvements. Oxygen system detail changes. Instrument vacuum system altered. Exhaust ducting modified.

P-47D-1-RE of 56th FG, May 1943. Externally similar to P47-C-2 and C-5, this variant had additional cowl flaps.

Model	P-47D-2-RE	Power rating	2,000 hp
Quantity built	445	Other data similar to P-47D-1-RE	
AAF Serials	42-7958 to 42-8402		
Engine	R-2800-21		

Changes: Turbo shroud removed.

P-47D-2-RE. As D-1-RE with modified turbo-exhaust shroud. 42-8369 assigned to 61st FS, December 1943.

Model	P-47D-2-RA
Quantity built	200
AAF Serials	42-22364 to 42-22563
Engine	R-2800-21
Power rating	2,000 hp
Other data similar to P-47D-1-RE	

Remarks: Evansville, Indiana. Similar to P-47D-2-RE.

P-47D-2-RA. Green-nosed 359th FG aircraft over-ran while landing at Burtonwood, England, May 1944. Evansville-made and similar to D-1-RE

Model	P-47D-5-RE	Power rating	2,000 hp
Quantity built	300	Other data similar to P-47D-1-RE	
AAF Serials	42-8403 to 42-8702		
Engine	R-2800-21		

Changes: General Electric C-21 supercharger (rated at

ENGINEERING AND PERFORMANCE DATA

20,000 rpm but restricted to 18,250 rpm due to inadequate cooling). Oxygen and fuel system detail changes from D-2-RE. First production a/c with provision for water injection equipment with engine-driven water pump. Production installation of 2-point B-7 bomb shackle assembly bolted to fuselage crash-skids for use with auxiliary drop tank or 1 x 100, 250, 325 or 500 lb bomb.

Remarks: 42-8702, last aircraft on line, taken and completed as XP-47K.

P-47D-5-RE. Farmingdale Thunderbolt with provision for water injection and two-point belly shackles. Green nosed 359th FG machine. (AFM)

Model	P-47D-3-RA
Quantity built	100
AAF Serials	42-22564 to 42-22663
Engine	R-2800-21
Power rating	2,000 hp

Other data similar to P-47D-1-RE

Remarks: Evansville, Indiana. Similar to P-47D-2-RA. Detail changes to oxygen and fuel systems. Not to D-5-RE standard so intermediate block number used.

Model	P-47D-4-RA
Quantity built	200
AAF Serials	42-22664 to 42-22863
Engine	R-2800-21
Power rating	2,000 hp
Other data similar to P-47D-1-RE	

Changes: General Electric C-21 supercharger. Provision for water injection equipment. Not to D-5-RE standard so intermediate block number used.

Remarks: Evansville, Indiana. Similar to P-47D-3-RA.

P-47D-4-RA. First Evansville aircraft with provision for water injection and the new model supercharger. (Harold G. Martin)

Model	P-47D-6-RE
Quantity built	350
AAF Serials	42-74615 to 42-74964
Engine	R-2800-21
Power rating	2,000 hp
Other data similar to P-47D-1-RE	

Changes: Electrical system detail changes.

P-47D-6-RE, 42-74688, flown by Cpt Leroy Gover, 4th FG, exhibits the extra large underwing national insignia specially advised for the Thunderbolt as an aid to recognition by anti-aircraft gunners.

115

REPUBLIC P-47 THUNDERBOLT

Model		P-47D-10-RE
Quantity built		250
AAF Serials		42-74965 to 42-75214
Engine		R-2800-63
Power rating		2,000/2,300 hp
Propeller		Curtiss Electric 12 ft 2 in dia
Dimensions:	Span	40 ft $9\frac{5}{16}$ in
	Length	36 ft $1\frac{3}{16}$ in
	Height	14 ft $3\frac{5}{16}$ in
	Wing area	300 sq ft
Weights:	Empty	9,900 lb
	Gross	13,500 lb
	Max	15,000 lb
Speeds:	Max	433 mph at 30,000 ft
	Landing	104 mph
	Climb	7.2 min to 15,000 ft
		11 min to 20,000 ft
		15 min to 25,000 ft
		20 min to 30,000 ft
Service ceiling		42,000 ft
Fuel:	Internal	305 US gal
	External	200 US gal
Range:	Max	835 miles at 10,000 ft (3.8 hrs)
	Normal	400 miles at 25,000 ft (1.3 hrs)
Armament:		6 or 8 x 0.50-in mg with from 267 rpg to 425 rpg

Changes: R-2800-63 with water injection operated manually by switch on throttle lever. General Electric C-23 turbo-supercharger (20,000 rpm with 15 min overspeed rating at 22,000 rpm). Redesigned turbo cooling system. Oil and hydraulic system detail changes. Hydraulic flap equaliser eliminated. Introduction of cable charging of guns.

Remarks: P-47D-4, -5 and -6 had provision for water injection and engines could be quickly modified. P-47C-2 and C-5, and P-47D-1, -2 and -3 could be modified but required 200 hrs work on each aircraft to effect.

P-47D-10-RE. Factory installation of R-2800-63 incorporating water injection. Orange tailed 42-75432 was operated by 358th FG, Germany, April 1945.

Model	P-47D-11-RE
Quantity built	400
AAF Serials	42-75215 to 42-75614
Engine	R-2800-63
Power rating	2,000/2,300 hp

Other data as P-47D-10-RE

Changes: Electrically-driven water pump automatically operated by throttle lever.

P-47D-11-RE differed from D-10-RE in operation of water injection pump. Photo clearly shows spine and cockpit contours. (Republic)

Model	P-47D-11-RA
Quantity built	250
AAF Serials	42-22864 to 42-23113
Engine	R-2800-63
Power rating	2,000/2,300 hp
Other data similar to P-47D-11-RE	

Remarks: Evansville, Indiana, standardisation with Farmingdale. On 42-23083 and following aircraft over-run on gun camera could be controlled by pilot.

P-47D-11-RA at Ontario, California, in May 1946 after retirement from military service. This block introduced operation of water injection when the throttle lever was pushed forward into its last half inch of travel. (W. T. Larkins)

Model	P-47D-15-RE
Quantity built	496
AAF Serials	42-75615 to 42-75864,
	42-76119 to 42-76364
Engine	R-2800-63
Power rating	2,000/2,300 hp
Other data similar to P-47D-11-RE	

Remarks: Production installation of wing pylons allowing a drop tank or bomb to be carried under each wing in addition to stores on the 'belly' shackles. Maximum internal tankage increased to a total of 375 US gal. Fuel system changes to incorporate plumbing, etc., for tanks on wing pylons. Production use of vacuum pump for drop tank feed pressure. Bomb selection and load increased: 2 x 1,000 lb or 3 x 500 lb; or other alternatives. Maximum bomb load: 2,500 lb. (Earlier P-47C and D models could be modified to receive wing racks). Jettisonable canopy.

P-47D-15-RE. Internal fuel tankage increased by enlargement of forward tank. First production with wing pylons for external stores. 42-76248 of 406th FG carries 2 × 500 lb bombs. The aircraft was wrecked a few days after this photo was taken in August 1944.

Model	P-47D-15-RA
Quantity built	157*
AAF Serials	42-23143 to 42-23299*
Engine	R-2800-63
Power rating	2,000/2,300 hp
Other data similar to P-47D-11-RE	

Remarks: Evansville. Changes similar to P-47D-15-RE. *42-23297 and 42-23298 later modified to become XP-47Hs.

P-47D-15-RA. Evansville production standardised with Farmingdale. 42-23194 of 33rd FG in China, August 1944, has been modified to take a D/F aerial. (USAF)

Model	P-47D-16-RE	Engine	R-2800-63
Quantity built	254	Power rating	2,000/2,300 hp
AAF Serials	42-75865 to 42-76118	Other data similar to P-47D-11-RE	

REPUBLIC P-47 THUNDERBOLT

Changes: Provision for use of 100/150 grade fuel and detail changes to fuel system.

P-47D-16-RE could use the higher octane fuels available in 1944.

Model	P-47D-16-RA
Quantity built	29
AAF Serials	42-23114 to 42-23142
Engine	R-2800-63

Power rating   2,000/2,300 hp
Other data similar to P-47D-11-RE

Remarks: Evansville. Changes similar to P-47D-16-RE

Model	P-47D-20-RE
Quantity built	300
AAF Serials	42-76365 to 42-76614
	42-25274 to 42-25322
Engine	R-2800-59
Power rating	2,000/2,300 hp
Other data similar to P-47D-11-RE	

Changes: Engine change. R-2800-59, as -21 and -63 but including General Electric ignition system. Longer tail wheel leg. Alterations in wing pylon tail. New model dynamotor, new radio jack box. Ducted heat to gun bays to replace electrical heating. Cockpit heating change. Revision of water injection switch operation.

Remarks: The 250th D-20-RE, 42-76614, taken from line and completed as XP-47L. Camouflage eliminated with 42-25274.

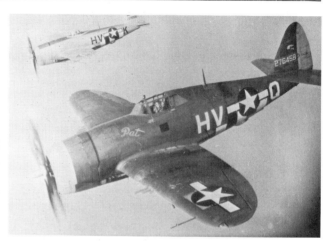

P47-D-20-RE introduced the R-2800-59 with new ignition equipment. Red nosed, red rudder aircraft of 61st FS, July 1944.

Model	P-47D-20-RA
Quantity built	187
AAF Serials	43-25254 to 43-25440
Engine	R-2800-59
Power rating	2,000/2,300 hp
Other data similar to P-47D-11-RE	

Remarks: Evansville. Changes similar to P-47D-20-RE.

P-47D-20-RA. Same changes as 20-RE. 43-25429 was assigned to the 19th FS, 318th FG, Saipan, July 1944.

Model	P-47D-21-RE
Quantity built	216
AAF Serials	42-25323 to 42-25538
Engine	R-2800-59
Power rating	2,000/2,300 hp

Other data similar to P-47D-11-RE

Changes: Manual operation of water injection via button-switch on throttle lever. Revised throttle quadrant.

Model	P-47D-21-RA
Quantity built	224
AAF Serials	43-25441 to 43-25664
Engine	R-2800-59

Power rating   2,000/2,300 hp
Other data similar to P-47D-11-RE

Remarks: Evansville. Changes as P-47D-21-RE.

ENGINEERING AND PERFORMANCE DATA

P-47D-21-RA, 43-25463, about to be lifted so that main wheels can be lowered. Underwing tanks took some of the impact when the undercarriage failed at Eagle Farm depot, Brisbane, 24 July 1944. (W. Bodie collection).

Model	P-47D-22-RE		
Quantity built	850		
AAF Serials	42-25539 to 42-26388		
Engine	R-2800-59		
Power rating	2,000/2,300 hp		
Propeller	Hamilton Standard Hydromatic 24E50-65, 13 ft $1\frac{7}{8}$ in dia		
Dimensions:	Span	40 ft $9\frac{5}{16}$ in	
	Length	35 ft 10 in	
	Height	14 ft $9\frac{1}{8}$ in dia	
	Wing area	300 sq ft	
Weights:	Empty	9,900 lb	
	Gross	13,500 lb	
	Max	15,000 lb	
Speeds:	Max	435 mph at 30,000 ft	
	Landing	104 mph	
	Climb	5.6 min to 15,000 ft	
		7.6 min to 20,000 ft	
		9.8 min to 25,000 ft	
		12.8 min to 30,000 ft	
Service ceiling		42,000 ft	
Fuel:	Internal	305 US gal	
	External max	375 US gal	
Range:	Max	835 miles at 10,000 ft (3.8 hrs)	
	Normal	400 miles at 25,000 ft (1.3 hrs)	
Armament:		6 or 8 x 0.50-in mg with from 267 to 425 rpg	
Bombs:		2 x 1,000 lb or 3 x 500 lb or 3 x 250 lb, etc. Max load 2,500 lb	

Changes: Propeller change. Hamilton Standard Hydromatic 13 ft $1\frac{7}{8}$ in paddle blade type. A-23 model turbo-regulator installed. Provision for carburettor heating eliminated with 42-25628.

P-47D-22-RE. Hamilton Standard paddle blade propeller fitted to this model had blunter nosed boss than Curtiss types. (Republic)

Model	P-47D-23-RA	Propeller	Curtiss Electric C542S 13 ft 0 in dia
Quantity built	889		
AAF Serials	43-25665 to 43-25753, 42-27389 to 42-28188	Dimensions: Span	40 ft $9\frac{5}{16}$ in
		Length	36 ft $1\frac{3}{4}$ in
Engine	R-2800-59	Height	14 ft $8\frac{1}{16}$ in
Power rating	2,000/2,300 hp	Wing area	300 sq ft

119

REPUBLIC P-47 THUNDERBOLT

Weights: Empty   9,900 lb
           Gross   14,000 lb
           Max   17,000 lb
Speeds: Max   426 mph at 30,000 ft
           Landing   106 mph
           Climb   6 min to 15,000 ft
                     8.1 min to 20,000 ft
                     10.5 min to 25,000 ft
                     13.5 min to 30,000 ft
Service ceiling   40,000 ft
Fuel: Internal 305 US gal

           External 375 US gal
Range: Max   800 miles at 10,000 ft (4.2 hrs)
           Normal   390 miles at 25,000 ft
Armament: 6 or 8 x 0.50-in mg with from
                     267 to 425 rpg
Bombs: 2 x 1,000 lb or 3 x 500 lb, etc
                     Max load 2,500 lb

Changes: New propeller. 13 ft Curtiss paddle-blade type with Type 836 blades. A-23 model turbo-regulator. Provision for carburettor heating deleted with 42-27559.

P-47D-23-RA. Apart from Curtiss propeller with paddle blades this model was similar to D-22-RE. White nosed example operated by 89th FS, 80th FG photographed on a dusty Burmese airstrip. (K. Sumney)

P-47D-25-RE was originally scheduled for production as P-47L. Apart from 360 degree vision canopy the D-25-RE had additional fuel tankage and oxygen.

Model	P-47D-25-RE	
Quantity built	385	
AAF Serials	42-26389 to 42-26773	
Engine	R-2800-59	
Power rating	2,000/2,300 hp	
Propeller	Hamilton Standard Hydromatic 25E50 13 ft 1$\frac{7}{8}$ in dia	
Dimensions:	Span	40 ft 9$\frac{5}{16}$ in
	Length	35 ft 10 in
	Height	14 ft 9$\frac{1}{8}$ in
	Wing area	300 sq ft

Weights: Empty   10,000 lb
           Gross   14,600 lb
           Max   17,500 lb
Speeds: Max   429 mph at 30,000 ft
           Landing   106 mph
           Climb   6.2 min to 15,000 ft
                     8.5 min to 20,000 ft
                     11 min to 25,000 ft
                     14 min to 30,000 ft
Service ceiling   42,000 ft
Fuel: Internal 370 US gal

ENGINEERING AND PERFORMANCE DATA

	External	410 US gal
Range:	Max	1,030 miles at 10,000 ft (5.3 hrs)
	Normal	590 miles at 25,000 ft
Armament:		6 or 8 x 0.50-in mg with from 267 to 425 rpg
Bombs:		2 x 1,000 lb etc. Max load 2,500 lb

Changes: 360° vision 'bubble' canopy. Cut down rear fuselage. Canopy electrically operated. Flat windshield.

Increased oxygen. Two extra bottles in rear fuselage (each 720 cu ft oxygen 450 lb/sq in. Cockpit layout changes, repositioned oil cooler shutter switch; repositioned toggle switch for intercooler. Turbo-tachometer. Larger main tank with 270 US gal capacity. Water tank capacity increased to 30 gal with reversion to engine-driven water pump. Radio equipment changes. Hydraulic fluid filtering introduced.

Remarks: Originally scheduled for production as P-47L.

Model	P-47D-26-RA
Quantity built	250
AAF Serials	42-28189 to 42-28438
Engine	R-2800-59
Power rating	2,000/2,300 hp
Propeller	Curtiss Electric 13 ft 0 in dia
Dimensions: Span	40 ft 9$\frac{5}{16}$ in
Length	36 ft 1$\frac{3}{4}$ in
Height	14 ft 8$\frac{1}{16}$ in
Wing area	300 sq ft
Weights: Empty	10,000 lb
Gross	14,500 lb
Max	17,500 lb
Speeds: Max	423 mph at 30,000 ft
Landing	105 mph

Climb	6.2 min to 15,000 ft
	8.5 min to 20,000 ft
	11 min to 25,000 ft
	14 min to 30,000 ft
Service ceiling	42,000 ft
Fuel: Internal	370 US gal
External	410 US gal
Range: Max	1,030 miles at 10,000 ft (5.3 hrs)
Normal	590 miles at 25,000 ft
Armament:	6 or 8 x 0.50-in mg with from 267 to 425 rpg. Max bomb load 2,500 lb

Remarks: Evansville. Changes similar to P-47D-25-RE apart from propeller.

P-47D-26-RA. First Evansville bubble canopy. 42-28382 was camouflaged in two shades of grey by 61st FS in England, August 1944.

P-47D-27-RE had improvements to engine accessories. 42-27105 in the yellow and red colours of 314th FS, 324th FG, France, March 1945.

REPUBLIC P-47 THUNDERBOLT

Model   P-47D-27-RE
Quantity built   615
AAF Serials   42-26774 to 42-27388
Engine   R-2800-59
Power rating   2,000/2,430 hp
Propeller   Hamilton Standard Hydromatic
               24E50 13 ft $1\frac{7}{8}$ in dia
Other data similar to P-47D-25-RE

Changes: With a/c 42-27074 power rating increased by 64 hp without and 130 hp with water injection. New engine starter. Improved drop tank control.

Remarks: 42-27385, 42-27386 and 42-27388 taken from line and completed as YP-47Ms. 42-27387 taken from line and completed as XP-47N.

Model   P-47D-28-RE
Quantity built   750
AAF Serials   44-19558 to 44-20307
Engine   R-2800-59
Power rating   2,000/2,430 hp
Propeller   Curtiss Electric C542S-A114
               13 ft 0 in dia
Other data similar to P-47D-25-RE

Changes: Propeller change from Hamilton to Curtiss paddle-blade type giving length change to 36 ft $1\frac{3}{4}$ in. Relocation of external stores controls in cockpit. Detail changes in hydraulics. Detail radio changes. Provision for radio compass.

P-47D-28-RE had several detail changes and introduced Curtiss paddle blade propellers to Farmingdale production thus again standardising with Evansville. This aircraft was assigned to 104th FS Maryland ANG in 1950. (Via David Menard)

Model   P-47D-28-RA
Quantity built   1,028
AAF Serials   42-28439 to 42-29466
Engine   R-2800-59
Power rating   2,000/2,430 hp

Propeller   Curtiss Electric C542S-A114
               13 ft 0 in dia
Other data similar to P-47D-26-RA

Remarks: Evansville. Changes similar to P-47D-27-RE.

P-47D-28-RA incorporated the same detail changes as the D-28-RE. This example served with the 64th FS, 57th FG in Italy, 1945, and was fitted with a dorsal fin fillet 'in the field'. (AFM)

Model   P-47D-30-RE
Quantity built   800
AAF Serials   44-20308 to 44-21107
Engine   R-2800-59
Power rating   2,000/2,430 hp
Propeller   Curtiss Electric C-542S-A114
               113 ft 0 in dia
Other data similar to P-47D-25-RE

Changes: Blunt nosed ailerons introduced. Revised gun camera mount and elimination of camera over-run control. Elimination of ring and bead gunsight. Electrical release mechanism for external stores. Permanent sway braces for external stores. Instrument changes. Dive flaps at 30 per cent of chord from leading edge of each wing. Detail changes in fuel line plumbing for external wing tanks. Detail changes in hydraulic oil filtering. Introduction of rearview mirror for bubble canopy.

ENGINEERING AND PERFORMANCE DATA

P-47D-30-RE. Most notable change in this series was the use of blunt nosed ailerons to improve control at very high speeds. Several were supplied to the French. (ECP Armées)

Model	P-47D-30-RA
Quantity built	1,800
AAF Serials	44-32668 to 44-33867, 44-89684 to 44-90283
Engine	R-2800-59
Power rating	2,000/2,430 hp
Propeller	Curtiss Electric C-542S 13 ft 0 in dia

Other data similar to P-47D-26-RA

Remarks: Evansville. Changes similar to P-47D-30-RE.

P-47D-30-RA. More Evansville D-30s were produced than any other block of Thunderbolts – 1,800. 44-33044 was operated by 526th FS, 86th FG at Neubiberg, last USAF unit in Europe with the P-47. (A. Pearcy)

Model	P-47D-40-RA
Quantity built	665
AAF Serials	44-90284 to 44-90483, 45-49090 to 45-49554
Engine	R-2800-59
Power rating	2,000/2,430 hp
Propeller	Curtiss Electric C-542S 13 ft 0 in dia

P-47D-40-RA. Last D model block had rocket mounting pylons and dive brakes under wings. Postwar, Col Robert Baseler had 45-49355 painted up in the markings of the 325th FG Thunderbolt he had flown in Italy in 1944. (AFM)

Other data similar to P-47D-26-RA

Changes: Dorsal fin as factory installation. K-14 gunsight

REPUBLIC P-47 THUNDERBOLT

in place of Mk VIII. Provision for zero-rail launchers (5 each wing). Shielding of induction vibrator and primary ignition leads. Installation of landing gear warning horn and lights. Tail warning radar.

Remarks: The new gunsight, rocket provisions, tail radar and landing gear warning system were originally planned for introduction with P-47D-35-RA, 44-33868. This aircraft was not built. The zero-length rocket launchers could be fitted on earlier models and 2850 kits were produced for service installation.

Model	XP-47E	
Quantity built	1	
AAF Serial	41-6065	
Engine	R-2800-21 and R-2800-59	
Power rating	2,000/2,300 hp	
Propeller	Curtiss Electric 12 ft 2 in dia, later Hamilton Hydromatic 13 ft 1 $\frac{7}{8}$ in dia	
Dimensions: Span	40 ft 9 $\frac{5}{16}$ in	
Length	35 ft 5 $\frac{3}{16}$ in	
Height	14 ft 2 in	
Wing area	300 sq ft	
Weights: Empty	9,350 lb	
Gross	12,250 lb	
Speeds: Max	429 mph at 28,000 ft	
Landing	92 mph	
Fuel: Internal	305 US gal	

Remarks: Taken from P-47B line and completed as pressure cabin model for high altitude flight. Air intake for pressurising unit situated in left wing root. Aircraft much modified during life. Performance similar to standard P-47B but higher speeds obtained with new engine and propeller.

XP-47E photographed at Wright Field in the winter of 1943/44 after the installation of a -59 engine and Hamilton 24E50 propeller. The aircraft was unarmed.

Model	XP-47F
Quantity built	1
AAF Serial	41-5938
Engine	R-2800-21
Power rating	2,000/2,300 hp
Propeller	Curtiss Electric 12 ft 2 in dia
Dimensions: Span	42 ft 0 in
Length	35 ft 5 $\frac{3}{16}$ in
Height	14 ft 2 in
Wing area	322 sq ft
Weights:	Empty approx. 9,000 lb
Speeds:	Max attained, approx. 430 mph
Fuel:	Internal 305 US gal

Remarks: A P-47B rebuilt with laminar flow type wing. Completely new wing shape with increased span. No arma-

ment installed; aircraft purely experimental. Crashed and destroyed on 14 October 1943; pilot, Cpt A. McAdams, killed.

XP-47F in summer 1943.

ENGINEERING AND PERFORMANCE DATA

Model	P-47G-CU
Quantity built	20
AAF Serials	42-24920 to 42-24939
Engine	R-2800-21
Power rating	2,000 hp
Propeller	Curtiss Electric 12 ft 2 in dia

Dimensions:	Span	40 ft $9\frac{5}{16}$ in
	Length	36 ft $5\frac{3}{16}$ in
	Height	14 ft 2 in
	Wing area	300 sq ft
Weights:	Empty	9,900 lb
	Gross	13,500 lb
	Max	15,000 lb
Speeds:	Max	420 mph at 10,000 ft
	Landing	102 mph
	Climb	7.5 min to 15,000 ft
		12 min to 20,000 ft
		16 min to 25,000 ft
		22 min to 30,000 ft
Service ceiling		42,000 ft
Fuel:	Internal	305 US gal
	External	200 US gal

Range:	Max	835 miles at 10,000 ft
	Normal	400 miles at 25,000 ft
Armament:		6 to 8 x 0.50-in mg, 267 rpg normal

Remarks: Built by Curtiss at Buffalo. Similar to P-47C-RE. First pre-production aircraft, September 1942. Flap indicator on first five aircraft only. Provision for blind flying hood in all P-47G models.

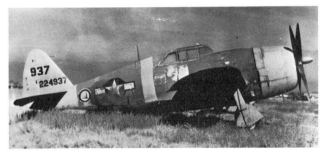

P-47G-CU. First production from Curtiss was equivalent to early P-47C. Yellow-tailed 42-24937 served as an Air Transport Command communications aircraft at one period.

Model	P-47G-1-CU
Quantity built	40
AAF Serials	42-24940 to 42-24979
Engine	R-2800-21
Power rating	2,000 hp
Other data similar to P-47G-CU	

Remarks: Similar standard to P-47C-1-RE. Length increased to 36 ft $1\frac{3}{16}$ in

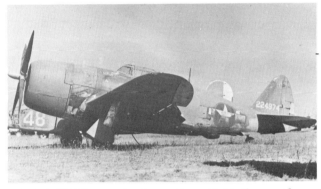

P-47G-1-CU. The extra fuselage section added to the rear of the engine accessories compartment can be clearly seen on 42-24974, which was modified during service and redesignated G-2-CU.

Model	P-47G-5-CU
Quantity built	60
AAF Serials	42-24980 to 42-25039
Engine	R-2800-21
Power rating	2,000 hp
Other data similar to P-47G-1-CU	

Remarks: Similar standard to P-47D-1-RE. Instrument vacuum system changes. Detail brake changes with aircraft 42-25008.

P-47G-5-CU. A test pilot prepares for a flight in an aircraft fresh from the Buffalo factory. (AFM)

125

REPUBLIC P-47 THUNDERBOLT

Model	P-47G-10-CU
Quantity built	80
AAF Serials	42-25040 to 42-25119
Engine	R-2800-21
Power rating	2,000 hp
Other data similar to P-47G-1-CU	

Remarks: Similar standard to P-47D-5-RE. B-7 two-point bomb shackles fitted.

P-47G-10-CU. Weatherbeaten veteran from US training bases. The bands encircling fuselage aft of aerial mast are a squadron commander's marking. (L. J. Cohn)

Model	P-47G-15-CU
Quantity built	154
AAF Serials	42-25120 to 42-25273
Engine	R-2800-63
Power rating	2,000/2,300 hp
Speeds: Max	430 mph at 30,000 ft
Landing	104 mph
Other data similar to P-47G-1-CU	

Remarks: Similar standard to P-47D-10-RE. Curtiss built

P-47G-15-CU, the largest block of Curtiss built Thunderbolts. 42-25234, painted in bogus markings, became a museum exhibit in the 1960s. (Roger Besecker)

P-47s were used principally in a training role. Two P-47G-15-CU (42-25267 and 42-25266) modified into experimental two-seat trainers. Main fuel tank reduced in size and second cockpit constructed above it. Cabin extended forward over new cockpit. These aircraft re-designated P-47G-16-CU. Curtiss production finished March 1944.

Model	XP-47H	
Quantity built	2	
AAF Serials	42-23297 and 42-23298	
Engine	Chrysler XI-2220-11	
Power rating	2,500 hp	
Propeller	Curtiss Electric 13 ft 0 in dia	
Dimensions: Span	40 ft 9$\frac{5}{16}$ in	
Length	38 ft 4$\frac{1}{4}$ in	
Height	13 ft 8 in	
Wing area	300 sq ft	
Weights: Empty	11,442 lb	
Gross	13,427 lb	

Speeds: Max	414 mph at 30,000 ft
Climb	2,800 ft per minute best
Service ceiling	36,000 ft
Fuel:	Internal 295 US gal
Range: Max	1,000 miles at 10,000 ft
Normal	700 miles at 25,000 ft
Armament:	Provision for 6 x 0.50-in mg but not installed

Remarks: Both aircraft originally as P-47D-15-RA. Purely engine test bed models for evaluation of Chrysler inverted-vee power plant. Entailed redesign of aircraft forward of

ENGINEERING AND PERFORMANCE DATA

firewall, new duct work to General Electric CH-5 turbo-supercharger and modifications to associated equipment, including intercooler outlet doors.

XP-47H. Purely engine test beds, the two examples were the only Thunderbolts powered by liquid-cooled engines. 42-23298, the second aircraft completed, was delivered to Wright Field in January 1946. (Republic)

Model	XP-47J	
Quantity built	1	
AAF Serials	43-46952	
Engines	R-2800-57 and R-2800-14W	
Power rating	2,100/2,800 hp	
Propeller	Curtiss Electric 13 ft 0 in dia	
Dimensions:	Span	40 ft 11½ in
	Length	35 ft 3 in
	Height	14 ft 3 in
	Wing area	300 sq ft
Weights:	Empty	9,663 lb
	Gross	12,400 lb
	Max	16,780 lb
Speeds:	Max	504 mph at 34,300 ft
	Landing	92 mph
	Climb	4.5 min to 15,000 ft
		4.25 min to 20,000 ft
Service ceiling	45,000 ft	
Fuel:	Internal	287 US gal
Range:	Max	1,070 miles at 10,000 ft
	Normal	765 miles at 25,000 ft
Armament:		6 x 0.50-in mg with 267 rpg

Remarks: With AAF testing XP-47J could not reach the top speed claimed by Republic. Aircraft superseded by XP-72 as high-performance interceptor project. Cooling fan for engine. More compact cowl. New model (CH-5) turbo-supercharger. Many detail changes and redesigned components aimed at reducing weight. Two prototypes and a static test airframe originally ordered. Plan to install contra-rotating propeller dropped.

XP-47J. Veins of the engine cooling fan are visible in this photograph as is the gun stagger arrangement – quite unlike that of any previous Thunderbolt. (Republic)

Model	XP-47K	
Quantity built	1	
AAF Serial	42-8702	
Engine	R-2800-21 and R-2800-59	
Power rating	2,000/2,300 hp	
Propeller	Curtiss Electric 12 ft 2 in dia	
Dimensions:	Span	40 ft 9 5/16 in later 42 ft 6 5/16 in
	Length	36 ft 1¾ in
	Height	14 ft 8 1/16 in
Weights:	Empty	10,000 lb
	Gross	14,000 lb (original configuration)
Speeds:	Max	415 mph at 30,000 ft (original configuration)
Fuel:	Internal	305 US gal
Armament:		6 or 8 x 0.50-in mg with 267 rpg

Remarks: Originally last P-47D-5-RE. Taken from line and extensively modified to take a 360° vision bubble canopy. Modification completed 3 July 1943. Subsequently reworked with long-range wing similar to that eventually produced for P-47N.

REPUBLIC P-47 THUNDERBOLT

XP-47K photographed in the summer of 1943. Originally a
P-47D, 42-8702 underwent extensive remodelling of the upper
fuselage to become the first bubble canopy Thunderbolt.
(Republic)

Model	XP-47L	Speeds:	Max	429 mph at 30,000 ft
Quantity built	1		Landing	106 mph
AAF Serial	42-76614	Fuel:	Internal	370 US gal
Engine	R-2800-21, later R-2800-59 and R-2800-57	Range:	Max	1,030 miles at 10,000 ft
			Normal	590 miles at 25,000 ft
Power rating	2,000/2,300 hp; 2,100 (2,800 hp with water injection)	Armament:		6 or 8 x 0.50-in mg with from 267 to 425 rpg
Propeller	Curtiss Electric 12 ft 2 in dia later 13 ft 0 in dia model			

Remarks: Originally last production P-47D-20-RE. Taken
from line for modification. Similar to XP-47K but with
main tank and detail changes. Put into production as
P-47D-25-RE. R-2800-C type engine installed at later date
for testing.

Dimensions:	Span	40 ft 9$\frac{5}{16}$ in
	Length	36 ft 1$\frac{3}{16}$ in
	Height	14 ft 8$\frac{1}{16}$ in
	Wing area	300 sq ft
Weights:	Empty	10,000 lb
	Gross	14,600 lb
	Max	17,500 lb

Model	YP-47M-RE
Quantity built	3
AAF Serials	42-27385, 42-27386, 42-27388
Engine	R-2800-14W and R-2800-57
Power rating	2,100/2,800 hp
Propeller	Curtiss Electric C642S-B40 13 ft 0 in dia
Dimensions: Span	40 ft 9$\frac{5}{16}$ in
Length	36 ft 1$\frac{3}{4}$ in
Height	14 ft 8$\frac{1}{16}$ in
Wing area	300 sq ft
Weights: Empty	10,340 lb
Gross	15,000 lb
Max	18,000 lb
Speeds: Max	473 mph at 32,000 ft
Landing	99 mph
Climb	13.4 min to 32,000 ft 5 min to 15,000 ft
Service ceiling	41,000 ft
Fuel: Internal	370 US gal
External	410 US gal
Range	530 miles at 26,000 ft
Armament:	6 or 8 x 0.50-in mg with 267 rpg

Remarks: Originally laid down as P-47D-27-RE but taken
from line and modified to test R-2800 'C' series engines and
new associated components. New CH-5 turbo-
supercharger. Unilever Power Control unit fitted giving
single lever control of boost, propeller and rpm.

The second YP-47M, 42-27386, on test at Farmingdale. Drop
tank is standard US metal unit of 110 gallon capacity. Yellow
empenage and cowling distinguished experimental P-47s at
Republic during 1944 and 1945. (Republic)

Model	P-47M-1-RE	Propeller	Curtiss Electric C642S-B40 13 ft 0 in dia
Quantity built	130		
AAF Serials	44-21108 to 44-21237	Other data similar to YP-47M
Engine	R-2800-57	
Power rating	2,100/2,800 hp	*Changes* (from P-47D-30-RE): New engine with increased

power. CH-5 model turbo-supercharger with C-1 type regulator (model 30-PR8-B2) giving greater capacity and better efficiency. Automatic manifold pressure switch for water injection. Electric fuel primer, shielding of induction vibrator and primary ignition leads. Planned Unilever

Power Control unit not installed.

Remarks: Basically high-power version of P-47D-30-RE. All aircraft sent to the 56th FG in UK. Dorsal fin fitted in the UK.

P-47M-1-RE. Basically a D model airframe with C model engine, the P-47M was the fastest of all production Thunderbolts. 42-1159, photographed at Newark, N.J. prior to being made ready for overseas shipment, was destroyed in a flying accident in March 1945 while operated by 62nd FS. (Harold G. Martin)

Model	XP-47N
Quantity built	1
AAF Serial	42-27387
Engine	R-2800-57
Power rating	2,100/2,800 hp
Propeller	Curtiss Electric C642S-B40 13 ft 0 in dia
Dimensions: Span	42 ft 10 in
Length	36 ft $1\frac{3}{4}$ in
Height	14 ft 6 in
Wing area	322.2 sq ft
Weights: Empty	10,988 lb
Gross	14,030 lb
Max	20,080 lb
Speeds: Max	467 mph at 32,000 ft
Landing	98 mph
Climb	13.5 min to 32,000 ft
Service ceiling	43,000 ft
Fuel: Internal	570 US gal
Range: Max	920 miles at 10,000 ft
Normal	800 miles at 25,000 ft
Armament:	6 or 8 x 0.50-in mg with from 267 to 425 rpg
Bombs: Max load	3,000 lb

Changes (from P-47D-30-RE): New Engine. Unilever Power Control. CH-5 model turbo-supercharger and regulator (as P-47M). New long-range wing with four interconnected self-sealing fuel cells in inboard section of each wing: 200 US gal total. Landing light and camera gun relocated. Oxygen wing bottle eliminated. Undercarriage tread increased to 18 ft $5\frac{13}{16}$ in. Modified undercarriage struts. New downlock cylinder in hydraulic system. 34 x 9.9

wheels and tyres. New brakes. Flap area increased to 46 sq ft. Aileron area to 27.97 sq ft. Oxygen capacity increased by 80%: total of seven oxygen bottles in rear fuselage. New collecting ring for exhaust system. Improved engine mount. New electrical generator. Automatic operation of cowl flaps by thermal-sensitive electric motors. New hydraulic unit for cowl flap power. Automatic cockpit heat control. Automatic operation of intercooler doors by thermal-sensitive electric motors. Automatic operation of water injection by manifold pressure sensitive switch (as P-47M). Oil tank capacity increased to 40 US gal. Relocation of electrical switches in cockpit.

Remarks: A P-47D-27-RE taken from line and reworked. Fuselage basically as P-47M. Only 80 of 100 US gal. in each wing fuel cells could be drawn on XP-47N.

XP-47N. Service prototype for the square-tipped long-range wing. (Republic)

REPUBLIC P-47 THUNDERBOLT

Model	P-47N-1-RE	
Quantity built	550	
AAF Serials	44-87784 to 44-88333	
Engine	R-2800-57	
Power rating	2,100/2,800 hp	
Propeller	Curtiss Electric C642S-B40 13 ft 0 in dia	
Dimensions: Span	42 ft 6$\frac{5}{16}$ in	
Length	36 ft 1$\frac{3}{4}$ in	
Height	14 ft 6 in	
Wing area	322.2 sq ft	
Weights: Empty	10,988 lb	
Gross	13,823 lb	
Max	21,200 lb	
Speeds: Max	467 mph at 32,000 ft	
Landing	98 mph	
Climb	14.2 min to 25,000 ft 9 min to 15,000 ft	
Service ceiling	43,000 ft	
Fuel: Internal	556 US gal	

	External	700 US gal
Range:	Max	2,000 miles at 25,000 ft
	Normal	800 miles at 25,000 ft
Armament:		6 or 8 x 0.50-in mg with from 267 to 500 rpg
Bombs:	Max load	3 x 1,000 lb

Changes (from XP-47N): Unilever Power Control omitted. Replaced by Automatic Engine Control unit. Scintilla engine ignition system. New boost/propeller mixture/throttle control quadrant in cockpit. Modified fuel cells in wings giving total of 186 US gal. Provision for 300 US gal tank sway braces added to bottom of each wing panel. Landing gear cockpit warning system changes.

Remarks: Speed limit of 200 mph when 300 gal wing tanks installed. Fuel consumption 300 gal/hr at 2,800 hp, 92 gal/hr at 1,140 hp cruise. Max. 72 degrees hg manifold pressure at War Emergency power. At gross weight required 3,800 ft take-off run to clear 50 ft obstacle.

P-47N-1-RE. First N off the production lines, 44-87784, with nose and tail painted yellow to distinguish it as a test aircraft. (Republic)

Model	P-47N-5-RE
Quantity built	550
AAF Serials	44-88334 to 44-88883
Engine	R-2800-57 or R-2800-73
Power rating	2,100/2,800 hp
Other data similar to P-47N-1-RE	

Changes: Detail radio changes. Installation of zero (length) rail rocket launchers. Provision for quick removal of wing tank adaptors. Installation of tail warning radar AN/APS-13. Installation of General Electric C-1 autopilot. Revised rudder pedals. Catapult launching provision. General Electric ignition system (on R-2800-73 engine). Homing radar.

Remarks: No performance figures available but P-47N-5-RE was slightly heavier and slower than previous model.

P-47N-5-RE. Zero length rocket attachment points were introduced with this N block. 44-88613 has armament removed to improve handling.

Model	P-47N-15-RE	Engine	R-2800-73
Quantity built	200	Power rating	2,100/2,800 hp
AAF Serials	44-88884 to 44-89083	Other data similar to P-47N-1-RE	

130

ENGINEERING AND PERFORMANCE DATA

Changes: Installation of S-1 bomb rack in place of B-10 shackles. Pilot seat with arm rests. K-14A or K-14B gunsight in place of K-14. Turbo-tachometer and warning light for CH-5 turbo-supercharger eliminated. Automatic Engine Control unit omitted.

Remarks: The new bomb shackles, gunsight and provision for quick removal of wing pylons were originally scheduled for the P-47N-10-RE, commencing with aircraft 44-88534. Only the wing pylon change was made at this number and production continued as the P-47N-5-RE.

P-47N-15-RE had equipment changes with no external differences. 44-89072 collects snow during the winter of 1945–46. (W. Larkins)

Model	P-47N-20-RE
Quantity built	200
AAF Serials	44-89084 to 44-89283
Engine	R-2800-73 or R-2800-77
Power rating	2,100/2,800 hp
Other data similar to P-47N-1-RE	

Changes: Radio change. Installation of emergency fuel system. Provision for individual pressurising of jettisonable tanks. Aero-Tech manifold pressure switch replacing LM Persons model.

P-47N-20-RE featured further internal changes. 44-89238 was operated by the All Weather Flying Center in 1947. (Roger Besecker)

Model	P-47N-20-RA
Quantity built	149
AAF Serials	45-49975 to 45-50123
Engine	R-2800-73 or R-2800-77
Power rating	2,100/2,800 hp
Other data similar to P-47N-1-RE	

Remarks: Evansville. Similar to P-47N-20-RE. Revised cockpit floor with smooth rudder pedal track introduced with 45-50051. Production tailed-off in September 1945.

P-47N-20-RA. Evansville N models were basically as N-20-REs. An N-25-RA block was planned but never built. (David Menard)

P-47N-25-RE. Final Thunderbolt production block at Farmingdale. 44-89430 in service with Delaware National Guard carries no US national insignia, the practice of some units in the late 1940s to indicate state and not federal control.

Model	P-47N-25-RE
Quantity built	167
AAF Serials	44-89284 to 44-89450
Engine	R-2800-73 or R-2800-77 or R-2800-81

131

REPUBLIC P-47 THUNDERBOLT

Power rating 2,100/2,800 hp
Other data similar to P-47N-1-RE

Changes: Installation of Automatic Engine Controls, plus Boost Reset. General Electric C-1 unit (model 39PC1B2). Re-installation of autopilot. Revised cockpit floor with smooth rudder pedal track (from 44 89294). Redesigned tail wheel linkage. Auxiliary cockpit ventilation. (Not known if this item actually installed before production ceased.) Reinforced ailerons and flaps against rocket blast.

Remarks: Final Farmingdale production. Line ceased in October 1945, but a few examples not delivered to AAF until December. Automatic Engine Controls not available for installation on P-47N-15 and -20 during production.

Model		XP-72
Quantity built		2
AAF Serials		43-6598 and 43-6599
Engine		Pratt & Whitney R-4360-13
Propeller		Aero Products contra-rotating
Power rating		3,000 hp
Dimensions:	Span	40 ft 11 $\frac{7}{8}$ in
	Length	36 ft 7 $\frac{13}{16}$ in
	Height	14 ft 6 in
	Wing area	300 sq ft
Weights:	Empty	10,965 lb
	Gross	14,750 lb
Speeds:	Max	490 mph at 25,000 ft
	Landing	104 mph
	Climb	20,000 ft in 5 minutes

Fuel:	Internal	370 US gal
Range	Normal	1,200 miles
Armament:		6 x 0.50-in mg & 267 rpg

Remarks: Given a completely new model number as designed from the outset to take a new model engine. Engineering concept basically as XP-47J. First XP-72 flew 2 February 1944, using large four-blade propeller. Second XP-72 flew in July 1944, with contra-rotating propeller and written off in take-off crash during early tests. Mechanical two-stage supercharger in first prototype.

XP-72. The ultimate Thunderbolt. 43-6598 was first example with a conventional 4-blade propeller.

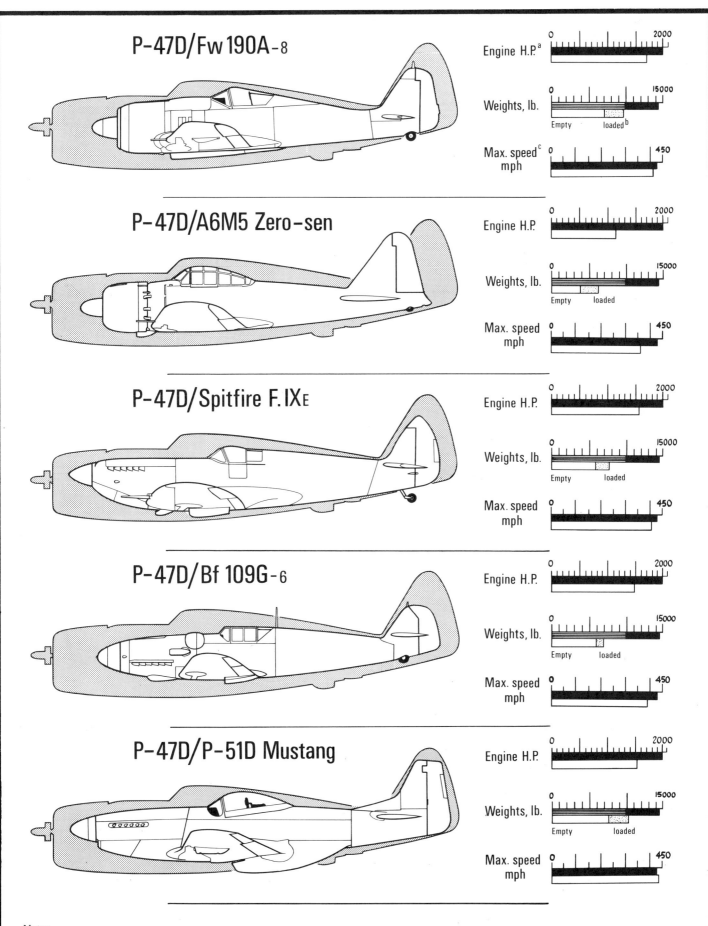

P-47D/Fw 190A-8

Engine H.P.[a] — scale 0 to 2000

Weights, lb. — scale 0 to 15000 (Empty, loaded[b])

Max. speed[c] **mph** — scale 0 to 450

P-47D/A6M5 Zero-sen

Engine H.P. — scale 0 to 2000

Weights, lb. — scale 0 to 15000 (Empty, loaded)

Max. speed mph — scale 0 to 450

P-47D/Spitfire F.IX E

Engine H.P. — scale 0 to 2000

Weights, lb. — scale 0 to 15000 (Empty, loaded)

Max. speed mph — scale 0 to 450

P-47D/Bf 109G-6

Engine H.P. — scale 0 to 2000

Weights, lb. — scale 0 to 15000 (Empty, loaded)

Max. speed mph — scale 0 to 450

P-47D/P-51D Mustang

Engine H.P. — scale 0 to 2000

Weights, lb. — scale 0 to 15000 (Empty, loaded)

Max. speed mph — scale 0 to 450

Notes
(a) The figure used in each case is horse-power available for take-off.
(b) External stores not included in loaded weight
(c) Max. speed quoted at the following altitudes: P-47, 30,000 ft.;

Fw190A-8, 20,800 ft.; A6M5, 22,000 ft.; Spitfire IX, 27,500 ft.;
Bf109G-6, 22,600 ft.; P-51D, 25,000 ft.
In each diagram the bar adjoining the scale indicates figure for P-47.

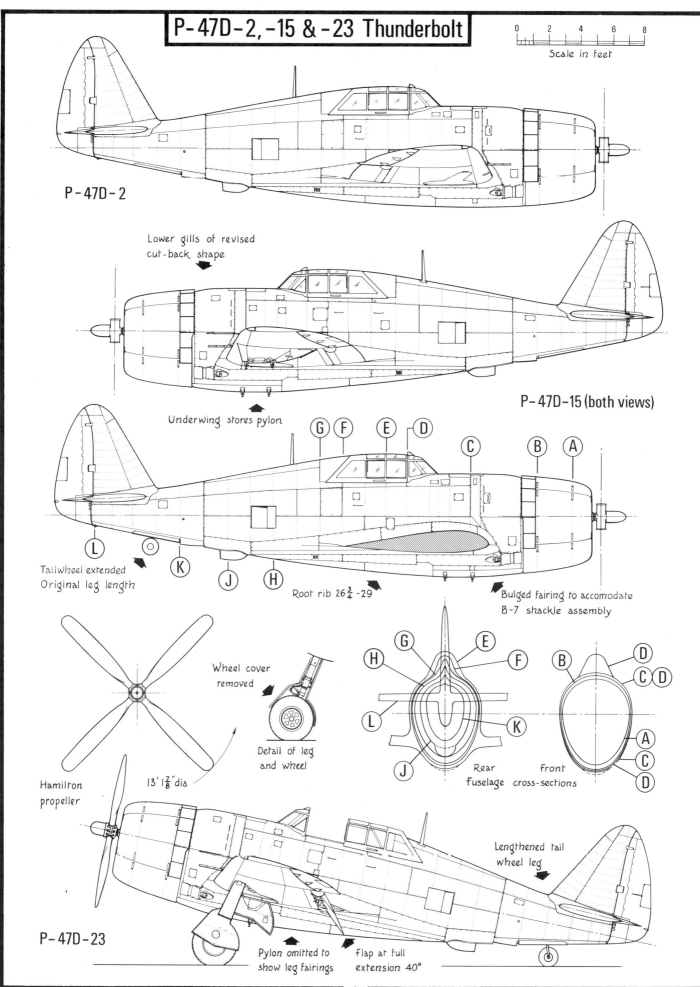

P-47D-2, -15 & -23 Thunderbolt

0 2 4 6 8
Scale in feet

P-47D-2

Lower gills of revised cut-back shape

P-47D-15 (both views)

Underwing stores pylon

G F   E   D   C   B A

Tailwheel extended
Original leg length

L   K   J   H

Root rib 26¾ -29

Bulged fairing to accomodate
B-7 shackle assembly

Hamilton propeller

13' 1⅞" dia

Wheel cover removed

Detail of leg and wheel

H G   E   F   B   D
                                    C D

L   K

J   Rear   Front   A
       Fuselage cross-sections   C
                                     D

P-47D-23

Lengthened tail wheel leg

Pylon omitted to show leg fairings

Flap at full extension 40°

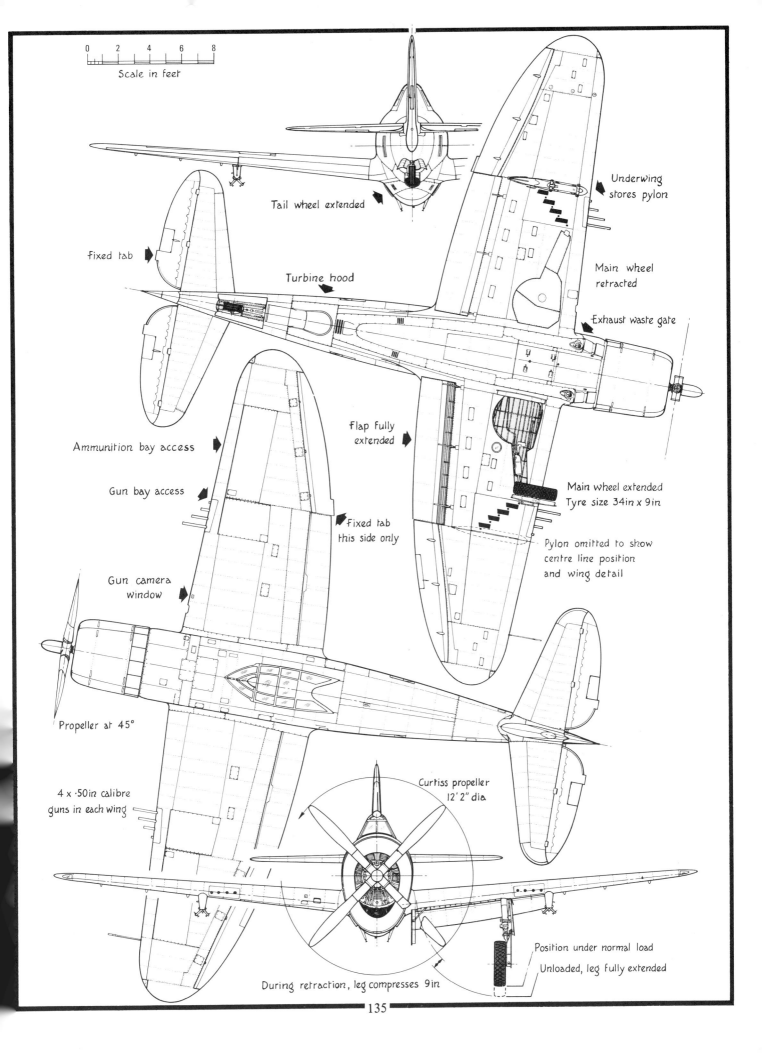

Scale in feet
0 2 4 6 8

Tail wheel extended

Underwing stores pylon

Fixed tab

Turbine hood

Main wheel retracted

Exhaust waste gate

Ammunition bay access

Flap fully extended

Gun bay access

Fixed tab this side only

Main wheel extended
Tyre size 34in x 9in

Gun camera window

Pylon omitted to show centre line position and wing detail

Propeller at 45°

Curtiss propeller
12' 2" dia

4 x ·50in calibre guns in each wing

Position under normal load

Unloaded, leg fully extended

During retraction, leg compresses 9in

135

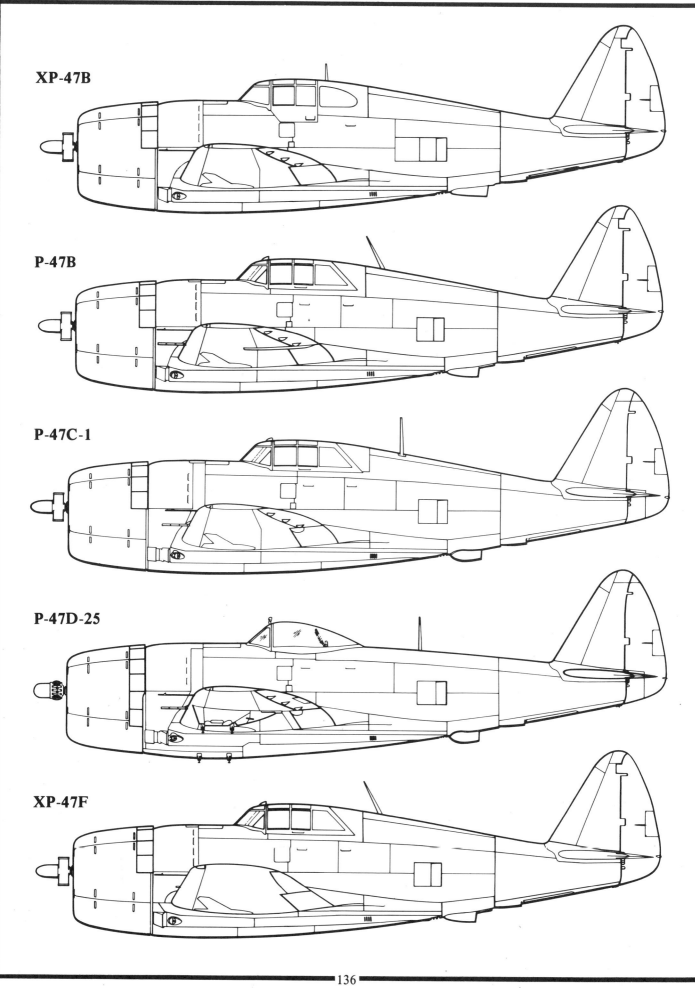

XP-47B

P-47B

P-47C-1

P-47D-25

XP-47F

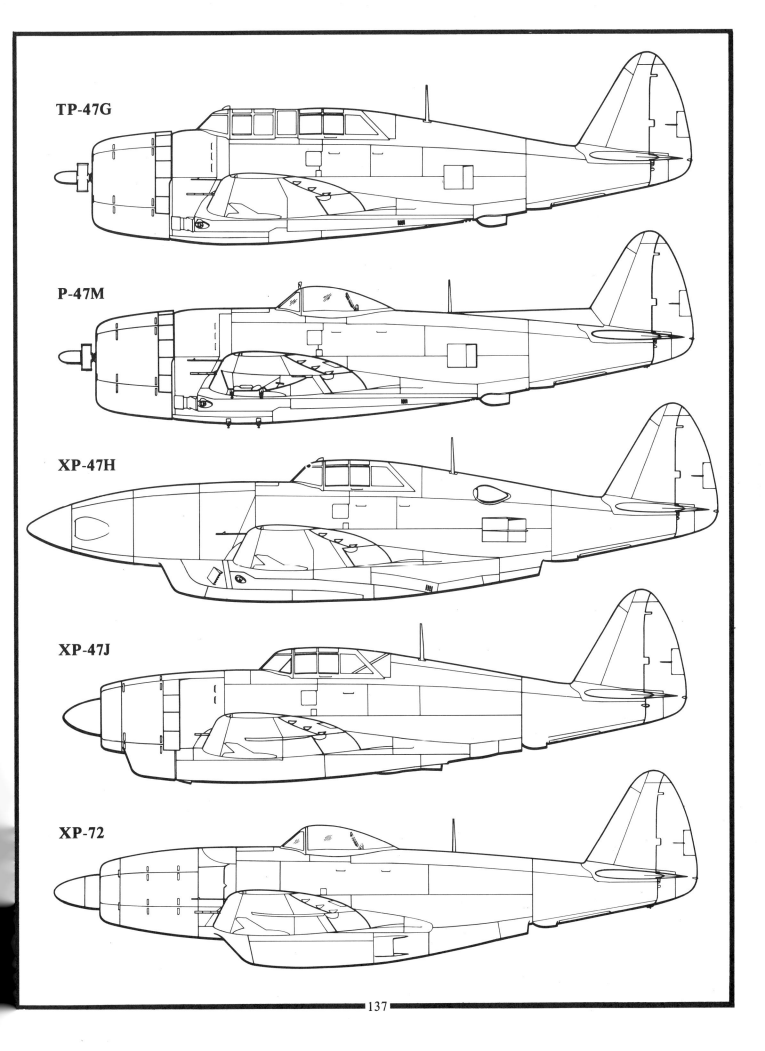

TP-47G

P-47M

XP-47H

XP-47J

XP-72

P-47N Thunderbolt

Curtiss 13ft dia paddle blade propeller

Leg position under normal load
Tyre size 34 in × 9.9 in

Leading edge profile revised outboard of this point

New wingtip

Aileron chord increased at outboard end

0 2 4 6 8
Scale in feet

Cut down rear fuselage and rear-view hood as on P-47D-25

18 in section inserted at wing root

Fuselage cross sections

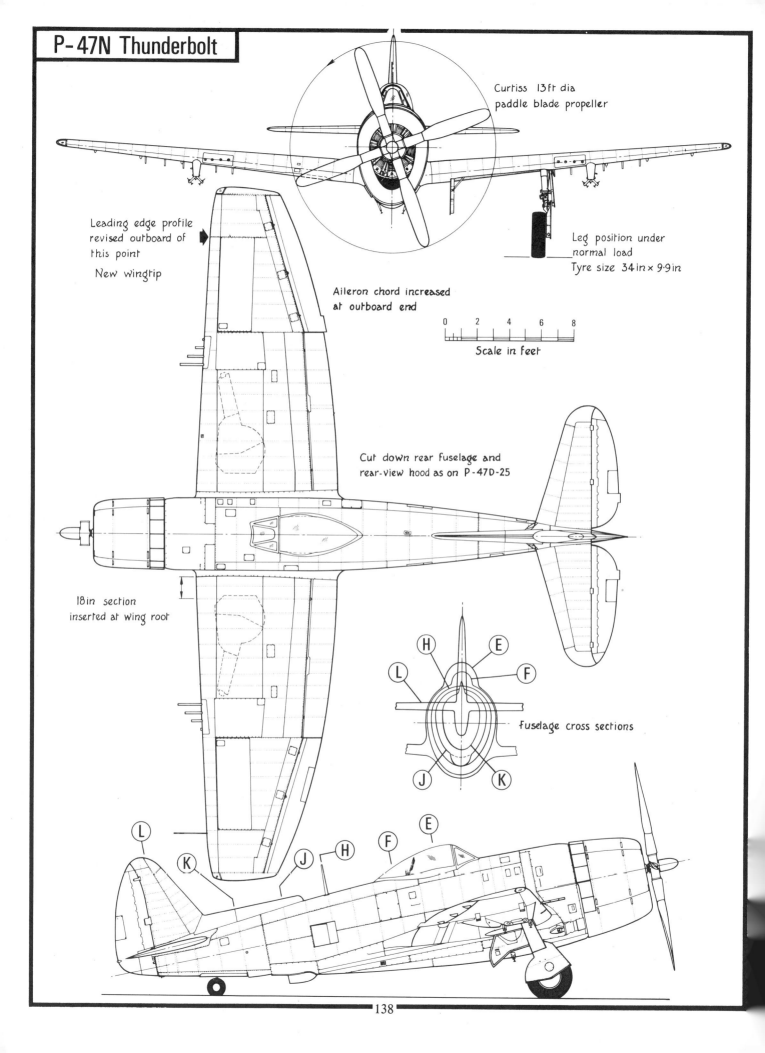

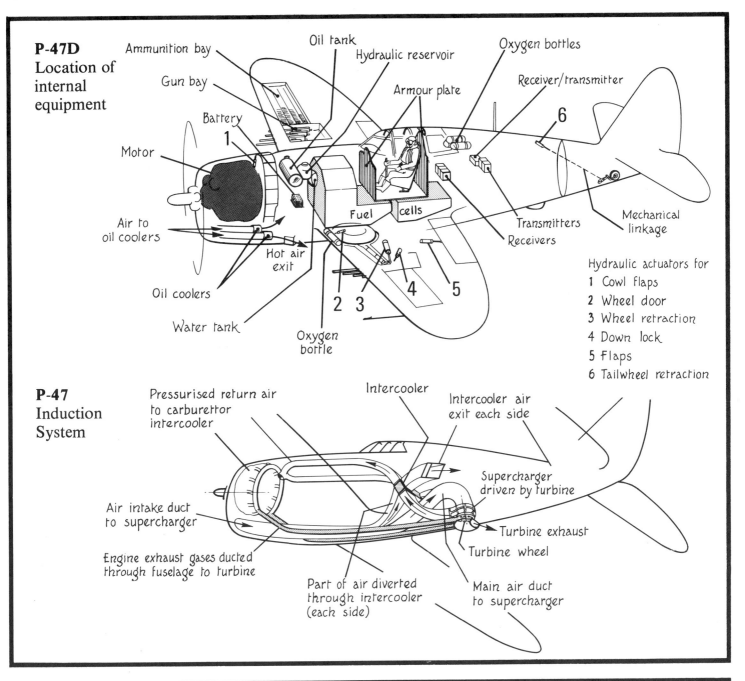

P-47D
Location of internal equipment

Ammunition bay
Gun bay
Motor
Battery
Oil tank
Hydraulic reservoir
Armour plate
Oxygen bottles
Receiver/transmitter
6
1
Air to oil coolers
Hot air exit
Oil coolers
Water tank
Oxygen bottle
2 3
4
5
Fuel cells
Transmitters
Receivers
Mechanical linkage

Hydraulic actuators for
1 Cowl flaps
2 Wheel door
3 Wheel retraction
4 Down lock
5 Flaps
6 Tailwheel retraction

P-47
Induction System

Pressurised return air to carburettor intercooler
Intercooler
Intercooler air exit each side
Air intake duct to supercharger
Engine exhaust gases ducted through fuselage to turbine
Part of air diverted through intercooler (each side)
Supercharger driven by turbine
Turbine exhaust
Turbine wheel
Main air duct to supercharger

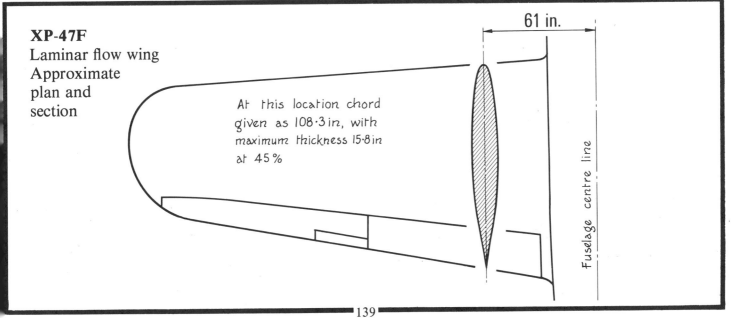

XP-47F
Laminar flow wing
Approximate plan and section

61 in.

At this location chord given as 108·3 in, with maximum thickness 15·8 in at 45%

Fuselage centre line

Fuselage and Wing Stations

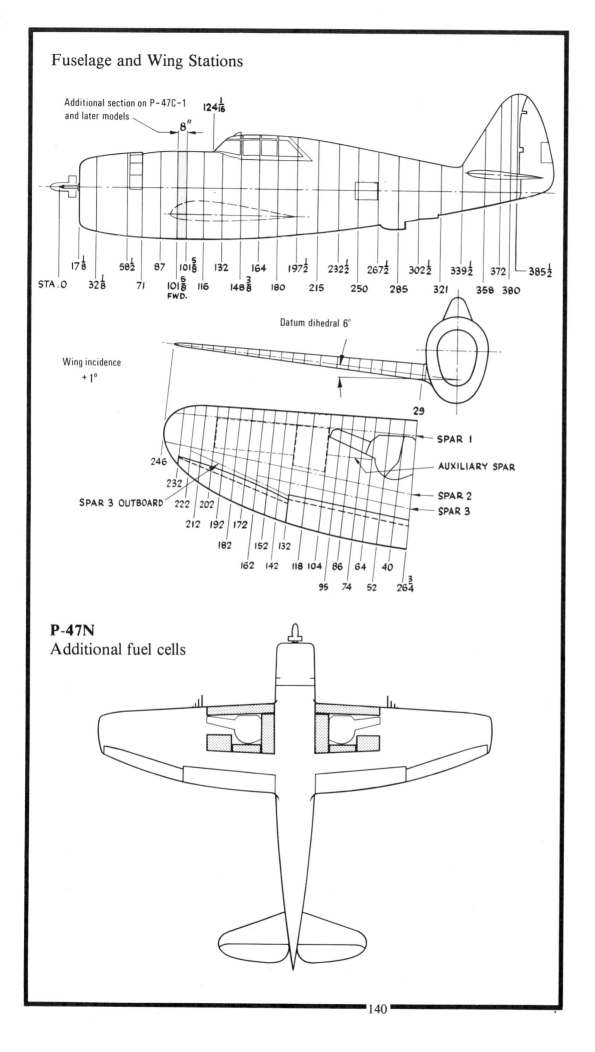

Additional section on P-47C-1 and later models

8"

$124\frac{1}{16}$

STA.0
$17\frac{1}{8}$
$32\frac{1}{8}$
$58\frac{1}{2}$
71
87
$101\frac{5}{8}$ FWD.
$101\frac{5}{8}$
116
132
$148\frac{3}{8}$
164
180
$197\frac{1}{2}$
215
$232\frac{1}{2}$
250
$267\frac{1}{2}$
285
$302\frac{1}{2}$
321
$339\frac{1}{2}$
358
372
380
$385\frac{1}{2}$

Datum dihedral 6°

Wing incidence + 1°

29

SPAR 1

AUXILIARY SPAR

SPAR 2

SPAR 3

SPAR 3 OUTBOARD

246
232
222
202
212
192
172
182
152
132
162
142
118
104
86
64
40
95
74
52
$26\frac{3}{4}$

P-47N
Additional fuel cells

14 Production Details

The total of 15,683 Thunderbolts built was the largest-ever production run for an American built fighter aircraft. Of these the majority came from the Farmingdale plant output of 9,087, with Evansville producing 6,242 and Curtiss 354. The average unit cost of a P-47 fell from $98,033 in 1942 to $84,897 in 1945 but these figures take into account development and other costs incurred in production. The cost of the aircraft as delivered was given as $82,997 for a P-47B in September 1942, $79,752 for a P-47D two years later, and $78,642 for a P-47N in January 1945.

The single XP-47B was built on contract AC 13817, approved 17 January 1940. No Republic airframe number is known. Farmingdale production was started with contract AC 15850, approved 13 September 1940. P-47B and P-47C models built to this contract received Republic airframe numbers 1 to 773. The first Farmingdale P-47Ds were on a new contract, AC 21080 for 850 aircraft, approved 14 October 1941. But from model P-47D-6-RE all following Farmingdale Thunderbolts were on contract 29279 approved 30 June 1942. With the introduction of the P-47D, constructors airframe numbers commenced at 1 again and continued through to 6645, the last basic D airframe (actually the final P-47M). P-47N production at Farmingdale also commenced at 1, and this serious ran to 1667. The XP-47F was funded through contract AC 19378 and the XP-47Js by AC 39160 approved 18 June 1943. The latter are believed to have been assigned Republic numbers J 1 and J 2. Other prototypes were based on adaptions of production airframes.

All Evansville Thunderbolts were built to a single contract, AC 24579 approved 31 January 1942 and airframe numbers ran 1 to 6242 irrespective of model changes. As far as is known the constructors' airframe numbers and AAF serials ran consecutively in numerical order. With the termination of production at Republic factories, orders for 5,934 P-47Ns were cancelled.

The Curtiss contract, AC 24545, was approved on the same date as that for Evansville but 4220 aircraft were cancelled and production was terminated at 354 units. Airframe numbers, in the Company's overall range, were 21814 to 22167.

15 The P-47 Power Unit
- the R-2800

The Pratt & Whitney R-2800 Double Wasp is a good candidate for the accolade 'Best radial aero-engine ever built'. Its reliability and durability was famous. 'Rugged', the favourite descriptive term among US pilots was a very valid one, too, in view of the number of severely battle-damaged 'twenty-eight hundreds' that did not fail. A good power/weight ratio earmarked this engine for no fewer than 141 different production aircraft types.

When first chosen to power the P-47 the R-2800 was still a comparatively new design and with only limited flight testing at high altitude. There were many engine failures in early Thunderbolts, generally resulting from the application of high manifold boost (via the turbo-supercharger) at high altitudes. The interrelation of boost, throttle and propeller pitch was critical if engine strain was to be avoided, but this was not fully appreciated in the early days of the P-47's service introduction. Basically, the R-2800 was extremely trouble-free and once the initial application problems of the two major models to the P-47 were overcome, it gave countless thousand hours of incident-free service. The B and C series were the maker's designations for the two major R-2800 models used in Thunderbolts.

Service identifications of model changes were by suffix numbers; those developed for the USAAF having odd numbers and those for the US Navy even numbers. The R-2800-11 was the engine originally specified for the XP-47B but the prototype first took to the air with the -17, a special one-off with experimental nose section and a torquemeter indicator. First R-2800 in production P-47s was identified as the R-2800-21 and following B series engines were basically the same. A notable advance was the addition of equipment to inject water into the intake manifold to keep cylinder temperatures down and allow higher power output for a limited period. This was known as War Emergency Power in AAF terminology. The R-2800-63 was the first factory-installed engine with water injection but all R-2800-21 models could be modified and, in combat theatres, usually were. When water injection was installed on a -21 engine it was redesignated as a

-63, and if further modified to receive a General Electric ignition system it became -59. The -35 was an experimental B engine fitted with the power section from an A series engine (a range for other aircraft) and fitted to XP-47B for a short period. B series engines were built by Pratt & Whitney at their Kansas City plant although Ford also built many -59 models.

Originally developed for a US Navy order, the C series engines used in later P-47s were more powerful without increases in piston displacement and only a minimal increase in weight. This was achieved by the redesign of many components to incorporate greater strength so as to withstand higher manifold pressures. A comparison can be gained from normal maximum manifold pressures specified for R-2800s in P-47s: 52 degrees hg with B engines and 55 degrees hg with C series. War Emergency Power was even more marked: 56 degrees B series and 72 degrees C series.

First C series engine tested in a Thunderbolt was a US Navy -14W. USAAF series models were -57, -73, -77 and -81 in service aircraft. The -57 was built both by Pratt & Whitney and Chevrolet and had Scintilla ignition equipment. The -73 was similar but with General Electric ignition, double acting propeller governor and was built only by Chevrolet. The -77 was only built by Chevrolet and was similar to the -73 but with Scintilla electrics. Pratt & Whitney built the -81 which was similar to the -57 but with General Electric cast ignition harness. A single special C type variant was the -61 built for the XP-47J but converted to a -57.

Perhaps the greatest tribute to the R-2800 was made by Dr Ing. Richard Vogt, head of the aircraft division of Blohm and Voss. He was so impressed by an example captured and tested by the Luftwaffe that he is quoted as pronouncing 'How could our leaders have ever dreamed of going to war against a nation which could afford to build such a beautiful engine for a warplane?' He particularly marvelled that the engine never became covered with oil, yet there were no internal seals between the power sections. The mating surfaces were lapped to such perfection that there was no seepage as was so common with other engines.

R-2800-59 'B' series

R-2800-63 'B' series

R-2800-57 'C' series

R-2800-73 'C' series

16 Thunderbolts for Allies

P-47s supplied to other nations during World War 2 were all from Army Air Force contacts. British, French, Soviet and Brazilian consignments were made at the factory although French and Brazilian units received additional aircraft from USAAF depots in combat areas. Thunderbolts used by the Mexican squadron in the Philippines were apparently supplied from local USAAF reserves.

Great Britain 919 allocated: 89 cancelled

Thunderbolt Mk I 240 allocated

USAAF Model	USAAF Serials	British Serials
P-47D-21-RE (2 aircraft)	Untraced	FL731 & FL732
P-47D-22-RE (238 aircraft)	42-25421 to 42-25438	FL733 to FL750
	42-25449 to 42-25488	FL751 to FL790
	42-25639 to 42-25678	FL791 to FL830
	42-25779 to 42-25818	FL831 to FL850
		HB962 to HB981
	42-25914 to 42-25953	HB982 to HB999
		HD100 to HD121
	42-26177 to 42-26236	HD122 to HD181

Thunderbolt Mk II 590 allocated

USAAF Model	USAAF Serials	British Serials
P-47D-25-RE (120 aircraft)	42-26477 to 42-26506	HD182 to HD211
	42-26593 to 42-26622	HD212 to HD241
	42-26722 to 42-26751	HD242 to HD271
	42-27885 to 42-26914	HD272 to HD301
P-47D-30-RE (420 aircraft)	44-19619 to 44-19658	KJ128 to KJ167
	44-19806 to 44-19845	KJ168 to KJ207
	44-19967 to 44-20006	KJ208 to KJ247
	44-20158 to 44-20197	KJ248 to KJ287
	44-20298 to 44-20337	KJ288 to KJ327
	44-20488 to 44-20527	KJ328 to KJ367
	44-20628 to 44-20657	KL168 to KL197
	44-20738 to 44-20797	KL198 to KL257
	44-20817 to 44-20846	KL258 to KL287
	44-20877 to 44-20906	KL288 to KL317
	44-20947 to 44-20976	KL318 to KL347
P-47D-30-RA (45 aircraft)	44-90076 to 44-90120	KL838 to KL886 range
P-47D-40-RA (1 aircraft)	44-90335	KL887

Four Mk IIs untraced

Farmingdale built aircraft were finished in standard RAF day fighter camouflage (dark sea grey and dark green shadow shading on upper surfaces; light grey under surfaces) at the factory. The final four batches were left in natural metal finish. While British records state that only 558 Thunderbolts were actually delivered, serial evidence indicates otherwise and that most of the 830 Thunderbolts prepared at the factories reached the RAF.

France

To equip units of the Free French Air Force raised in North Africa, several batches totalling 470 aircraft were allocated from factory production. Only 446 of these were delivered but many other P-47s were received direct from USAAF depots in Italy and France. In May 1945 the residue of the Thunderbolts serving with French units, 131 P-47Ds of several sub-models, were given to *L'Armée de l'Air*. The majority of French Thunderbolts were factory finished in camouflage colours – dark green upper surfaces and grey under surfaces.

Known factory allocations

USAAF Model	USAAF Serials
P-47D-4-RA (30 aircraft)	42-22808 to 42-22838
P-47D-22-RE (15 aircraft)	42-25819 to 42-25833
P-47D-25-RE (15 aircraft)	42-26508 to 42-26522
P-47D-27-RE (15 aircraft)	42-26870 to 42-26884
P-47D-28-RE (90 aircraft)	44-19669 to 44-19708
	44-20008 to 44-20057
P-47D-30-RE (140 aircraft)	44-20348 to 44-20387
	44-20658 to 44-20707
	44-20807 to 44-20816
	44-20907 to 44-20946
P-47D-30-RA (122 aircraft)	44-33369
	44-33376 to 44-33409
	44-33670 to 44-33697
	44-33701 to 44-33709

USAAF Serials
44-89787 to 44-89794
44-89796 to 44-89800
44-89802, 44-89803, 44-89806,
44-89807
44-89809 to 44-89815
44-89821, 44-89822, 44-89823,
44-89928, 44-89968, 44-89997,
44-90004, 44-90009, 44-90019,
44-90024, 44-90039, 44-90121,
44-90123, 44-90127, 44-90129,
44-90130, 44-90134, 44-90139,
44-90143, 44-90152, 44-90153,
44-90153, 44-90154, 44-90162,
44-90216, 44-90218

USSR 203 allocated. Soviet designation unknown.

USAAF Models	*USAAF Serials*
3 P-47D-10-RE	42-75201 to 42-75203
100 P-47D-22-RE	42-25539 to 42-25638
50 P-47D-27-RE	42-27015 to 42-27064
50 P-47D-27-RE	42-27115 to 42-27164

Only 196 Thunderbolts handed over as 7 were lost before delivery. The first three aircraft were sent via Alaska–Siberia, 4 went by ship to north Russia and the remainder were shipped to the Persian Gulf. Factory finish for these P-47s was the standard USAAF camouflage.

Brazil 88 allocated.
Several small batches taken chiefly from production blocks P-47D-25-RE, P-47D-27-RE, P-47D-28-RE and P-47D-30-RE. Farmingdale allocations finished with dark green upper surfaces and grey under surfaces.

Known allocations

USAAF Model	*USAAF Serials*
P-47D-25-RE	42-26753 to 42-26773
(21 aircraft)	
P-47D-27-RE	42-26774 to 42-26784
(15 aircraft)	42-26786 to 42-26789
P-47D-28-RE	44-19659 to 44-19668
(10 aircraft)	
P-47D-30-RE	44-20338 to 44-20347
(20 aircraft)	44-20798 to 44-20807

Note: A few aircraft within these ranges did not reach the Brazilians and were replaced with others.

Mexico 22 known P-47D-30 and -40
USSAAF Serials: 44-89945, 44-90008, 44-90049, 44-90165, 44-90170, 44-90180, 4490190, 44-90194, 44-90196, 44-90198, 44-90199, 44-90202, 44-90204, 44-90205, 44-90208 to 44-90211, 44-90214, 44-90215, 44-90217 and 44-90226.

US 8th & 9th Air Force Unit Identification Codes

AJ	356 FS	B2	390 FS
CH	365 FS	B4	387 FS
CP	367 FS	B7	374 FS
CR	370 FS	B8	379 FS
CS	370 FS	C2	396 FS
CV	368 FS	C4	388 FS
DQ	551 FS(?)	D3	397 FS
FT	353 FS	D5	386 FS
GQ	355 FS	E2	375 FS
HL	83 FS	E4	377 FS
HO	487 FS	E9	376 FS
HV	61 FS	F4	492 FS
IA	366 FS	G8	378 FS
IV	369 FS	G9	509 FS
IZ	Unknown	H5	392 FS
LA	2906 OTG(P)	I7	493 FS
		K4	511 FS
LH	350 FS	L3	513 FS
LJ	3 GTTFlt	O7	514 FS
LM	62 FS	R3	410 FS
MX	82 FS	T5	10 FS
OC	359 FS	U9	411 FS
OS	357 FS	V5	412 FS
PE	328 FS	W3	313 FS
PI	360 FS	Y8	507 FS
PZ	486 FS	2N	81 FS
QI	361 FS	2Z	510 FS
QP	334 FS	3T	22 FS
SX	352 FS	4K	506 FS
UN	63 FS	4N	394 FS
VF	336 FS	4P	512 FS
VM	552 FS(?)	4W	406 FS
VQ	8 ATSect	5F	5 ERS
WD	335 FS	6M	494 FS
WR	354 FS	6V	53 FS
WZ	84 FS	7J	508 FS
YF	358 FS	7U	23 FS
YJ	351 FS	8L	393 FS
A6	389 FS	8N	405 FS
A7	395 FS	9Q	404 FS
A8	391 FS		

Royal Air Force Thunderbolt Unit Identification Codes

AD	113 Sqdn	NX	131 Sqdn
AW	42 Sqdn	NV	79 Sqdn
EG	34 Sqdn	OQ	5 Sqdn
FJ	261 Sqdn	RS	30 Sqdn
FL	81 Sqdn	WA	146 Sqdn
GQ	134 Sqdn	WK	135 Sqdn
KW	615 Sqdn	XE	123 Sqdn
MU	60 Sqdn	ZT	258 Sqdn

17 Operational Squadrons
equipped with the Thunderbolt during World War 2

United States Army Air Forces

These tables give the unit, parent group, area of operations and the dates (month and year) of using P-47s in a combat theatre. The last date, if after May 1945, is also usually that of movement or disbandment of the unit. This listing does not include training squadrons or first-line squadrons operating in a defensive role outside combat areas.

US squadrons in some instances operated independently, but the majority were activated as components of a three-squadron group, usually remaining with that group throughout the war. An exception to the three-squadron rule was 348th FG which formed and operated an additional squadron from August 1944. Authorised unit establishment of a USAAF P-47 squadron was originally 25 aircraft. By the end of hostilities as many as 42, inclusive of spares, were permitted. However, the usual total strength of a squadron towards the end of 1944 was 30 to 35.

Abbreviations: ACG – Air Commando Group, FG – Fighter Group, FS – Fighter Squadron, FS(C) – Fighter Squadron (Commando), ERS – Emergency Rescue Squadron, CBI – China/Burma/India theatre, ETO – European Theatre of Operations, MTO – Mediterranean Theatre of Operations, PTO – Pacific Theatre of Operations.

Unit	Parent Group	Area of Operations	Active–Inactive	Model Used
1 FS	413 FG	PTO	5/45-10/46	P-47N
5 ERS		ETO	5/44-10/45	P-47D
5 FS(C)	1 ACG	CBI	9/44-5/45	P-47D
6 FS(C)	1 ACG	CBI	9/44-5/45	P-47D
9 FS	49 FG	PTO	11/43-4/44	P-47D
10 FS	50 FG	ETO	3/44-8/45	P-47D
19 FS	318 FG	PTO	6/44-12/45	P-47D&N
21 FS	413 FG	PTO	5/45-10/46	P-47N
22 FS	36 FG	ETO	4/44-2/46	P-47D
23 FS	36 FG	ETO	4/44-2/46	P-47D
33 FS		ETO	4/44-5/45	P-47D
34 FS	413 FG	PTO	5/45-10/46	P-47D
36 FS	8 FG	PTO	12/43-2/44	P-47D
39 FS	35 FG	PTO	12/43-3/45	P-47D

Unit	Parent Group	Area of Operations	Active–Inactive	Model Used
40 FS	35 FG	PTO	12/43-3/45	P-47D
41 FS	35 FG	PTO	12/43-3/45	P-47D
53 FS	36 FG	ETO	4/44-2/46	P-47D
58 FS	33 FG	CBI	4/44-10/45	P-47D
59 FS	33 FG	CBI	4/44-10/45	P-47D
60 FS	33 FG	CBI	4/44-10/45	P-47D
61 FS	56 FG	ETO	2/43-10/45	P-47C,D&M
62 FS	56 FG	ETO	2/43-10/45	P-47C,D&M
63 FS	56 FG	ETO	2/43-10/45	P-47C,D&M
64 FS	57 FG	MTO	1/44-8/45	P-47D
65 FS	57 FG	MTO	1/44-8/45	P-47D
66 FS	57 FG	MTO	1/44-8/45	P-47D
69 FS	58 FG	PTO	2/44-12/45	P-47D
73 FS	318 FG	PTO	6/44-12/45	P-47D&N
81 FS	50 FG	ETO	3/44-8/45	P-47D
82 FS	78 FG	ETO	2/43-12/44	P-47C&D
83 FS	78 FG	ETO	2/43-12/44	P-47C&D
84 FS	78 FG	ETO	2/43-12/44	P-47C&D
85 FS	79 FG	MTO	3/44-6/47	P-47D
86 FS	79 FG	MTO	3/44-6/47	P-47D
87 FS	79 FG	MTO	3/44-6/47	P-47D
88 FS	80 FG	CBI	5/44-10/45	P-47D
89 FS	80 FG	CBI	5/44-10/45	P-47D
90 FS	80 FG	CBI	5/44-10/45	P-47D
91 FS	81 FG	CBI	4/44-12/45	P-47D
92 FS	81 FG	CBI	4/44-12/45	P-47D
93 FS	81 FG	CBI	4/44-12/45	P-47D
99 FS	332 FG	MTO	4/44-6/44	P-47D
100 FS	332 FG	MTO	4/44-6/44	P-47D
301 FS	332 FG	MTO	4/44-6/44	P-47D
302 FS	332 FG	MTO	4/44-6/44	P-47D
310 FS	58 FG	PTO	2/44-12/45	P-47D
311 FS	58 FG	PTO	2/44-12/45	P-47D
313 FS	50 FG	ETO	3/44-8/45	P-47D
314 FS	324 FG	MTO	7/44-10/45	P-47D
315 FS	324 FG	MTO	7/44-10/45	P-47D
316 FS	324 FG	MTO	7/44-10/45	P-47D
317 FS	325 FG	MTO	11/43-5/44	P-47D
318 FS	325 FG	MTO	11/43-5/44	P-47D
319 FS	325 FG	MTO	11/43-5/44	P-47D
328 FS	352 FG	ETO	7/43-4/44	P-47D
333 FS	318 FG	PTO	6/44-12/45	P-47D&N
334 FS	4 FG	ETO	2/43-2/44	P-47C&D
335 FS	4 FG	ETO	2/43-2/44	P-47C&D
336 FS	4 FG	ETO	2/43-2/44	P-47C&D

Unit	Parent Group	Area of Operations	Active– Inactive	Model Used
340 FS	348 FG	PTO	6/43-3/45	P-47C &D
341 FS	348 FG	PTO	6/43-3/45	P-47C &D
342 FS	348 FG	PTO	6/43-3/45	P-47C &D
345 FS	350 FG	MTO	7/44-7/45	P-47D
346 FS	350 FG	MTO	7/44-7/45	P-47D
347 FS	350 FG	MTO	7/44-7/45	P-47D
350 FS	353 FG	ETO	7/43-10/44	P-47D
351 FS	353 FG	ETO	7/43-10/44	P-47D
352 FS	353 FG	ETO	7/43-10/44	P-47D
353 FS	354 FG	ETO	11/44-2/45	P-47D
354 FS	355 FG	ETO	7/43-4/44	P-47D
355 FS	354 FG	ETO	11/44-2/45	P-47D
356 FS	354 FG	ETO	11/44-2/45	P-47D
357 FS	355 FG	ETO	7/43-4/44	P-47D
358 FS	355 FG	ETO	7/43-4/44	P-47D
359 FS	356 FG	ETO	8/43-11/44	P-47D
360 FS	356 FG	ETO	8/43-11/44	P-47D
361 FS	356 FG	ETO	8/43-11/44	P-47D
365 FS	358 FG	ETO	10/43-7/45	P-47D
366 FS	358 FG	ETO	10/43-7/45	P-47D
367 FS	358 FG	ETO	10/43-7/45	P-47D
368 FS	359 FG	ETO	11/43-5/44	P-47D
369 FS	359 FG	ETO	11/43-5/44	P-47D
370 FS	359 FG	ETO	11/43-5/44	P-47D
374 FS	361 FG	ETO	12/43-5/44	P-47D
375 FS	361 FG	ETO	12/43-5/44	P-47D
376 FS	361 FG	ETO	12/43-5/44	P-47D
377 FS	362 FG	ETO	12/43-8/45	P-47D
378 FS	362 FG	ETO	12/43-8/45	P-47D
379 FS	362 FG	ETO	12/43-8/45	P-47D
386 FS	365 FG	ETO	12/43-9/45	P-47D
387 FS	365 FG	ETO	12/43-9/45	P-47D
388 FS	365 FG	ETO	12/43-9/45	P-47D
389 FS	366 FG	ETO	1/44-8/46	P-47D
390 FS	366 FG	ETO	1/44-8/46	P-47D
391 FS	366 FG	ETO	1/44-8/46	P-47D
392 FS	367 FG	ETO	2/45-7/45	P-47D
393 FS	367 FG	ETO	2/45-7/45	P-47D
394 FS	367 FG	ETO	2/45-7/45	P-47D
395 FS	368 FG	ETO	2/44-8/46	P-47D
396 FS	368 FG	ETO	2/44-8/46	P-47D
397 FS	368 FG	ETO	2/44-8/46	P-47D
404 FS	371 FG	ETO	3/44-10/45	P-47D
405 FS	371 FG	ETO	3/44-10/45	P-47D
406 FS	371 FG	ETO	3/44-10/45	P-47D
410 FS	373 FG	ETO	4/44-7/45	P-47D
411 FS	373 FG	ETO	4/44-7/45	P-47D
412 FS	373 FG	ETO	4/44-7/45	P-47D
413 FS	414 FG	PTO	7/44-9/46	P-47N
437 FS	414 FG	PTO	7/44-9/46	P-47N
456 FS	414 FG	PTO	7/44-9/46	P-47N
460 FS	348 FG	PTO	9/44-3/45	P-47D
463 FS	507 FG	PTO	6/45-5/46	P-47N
464 FS	507 FG	PTO	6/45-5/46	P-47N
465 FS	507 FG	PTO	6/45-5/46	P-47N
486 FS	352 FG	ETO	7/43-4/44	P-47D
487 FS	352 FG	ETO	7/43-4/44	P-47D

Unit	Parent Group	Area of Operations	Active– Inactive	Model Used
492 FS	48 FG	ETO	3/44-8/45	P-47D
493 FS	48 FG	ETO	3/44-8/45	P-47D
494 FS	48 FG	ETO	3/44-8/45	P-47D
506 FS	404 FG	ETO	4/44-8/45	P-47D
507 FS	404 FG	ETO	4/44-8/45	P-47D
508 FS	404 FG	ETO	4/44-8/45	P-47D
509 FS	405 FG	ETO	3/44-7/45	P-47D
510 FS	405 FG	ETO	3/44-7/45	P-47D
511 FS	405 FG	ETO	3/44-7/45	P-47D
512 FS	406 FG	ETO	4/44-8/46	P-47D
513 FS	406 FG	ETO	4/44-8/46	P-47D
514 FS	406 FG	ETO	4/44-8/46	P-47D
522 FS	27 FG	MTO	6/44-10/45	P-47D
523 FS	27 FG	MTO	6/44-10/45	P-47D
524 FS	27 FG	MTO	6/44-10/45	P-47D
525 FS	86 FG	MTO	6/44-3/46	P-47D
526 FS	86 FG	MTO	6/44-3/46	P-47D
527 FS	86 FG	MTO	6/44-3/46	P-47D

Royal Air Force

Authorised squadron establishment was 16 aircraft although there were often 20 on strength. All Thunderbolt squadrons served in the India-Burma theatre of operations.

Squadron	Active – Inactive	Mark
5	9/44-3/46	Thunderbolt I & II
30	7/44-12/45	Thunderbolt I & II
34	3/45-10/45	Thunderbolt II
42	6/45-12/45	Thunderbolt II
60	6/45-10/46	Thunderbolt II
79	7/44-12/45	Thunderbolt I & II
81	6/45-6/46	Thunderbolt II
113	4/45-10/45	Thunderbolt I & II
123 (became) 81	9/44-6/45	Thunderbolt I & II
131	6/45-12/45	Thunderbolt I & II
134 (became 131)	9/44-6/45	Thunderbolt I & II
135 (became 615)	6/44-4/45	Thunderbolt I & II
146 (became 42)	6/44-6/45	Thunderbolt I & II
258	9/44-12/45	Thunderbolt I & II
261	7/44-9/45	Thunderbolt I & II
615	6/45-9/45	Thunderbolt II

Brazilian Air Force (Forca Aérea Brasileira)

Only unit involved in combat operations was attached to the 350th Fighter Group, of US Twelfth Air Force, as a fourth Squadron. Unit establishment 25 a/c.

Unit	Active – Inactive	Model
1 Grupo de Caca	10/44-6/45	P-47D

Mexican Air Force (Fuerza Aérea Mexicana)

A single unit operated against the Japanese with the

147

USAAF Thunderbolt units were noted for their colourful markings. Here yellow and black paint is being applied by mechanics of 325th FG in Italy (checkerboard) and the 318th FG (stripes) on Ie Shima, Okinawa. On a French airfield the 387th BG (a B-26 unit) found two abandoned 511th FS P-47Ds from which a single flyable hack was built and adorned with the yellow and black Group marking as a nose band. (USAF and R. Western)

OPERATIONAL SQUADRONS IN WORLD WAR 2

US Fifth Air Force's 58th Fighter Group, acting as a fourth squadron. Unit establishment was 25 to 30 aircraft.

Unit	Active – Inactive	Model
201 Escuadron Aereo de Pelea	5/45-10/45	P-47D

FRENCH AIR FORCE (L'ARMÉE DE L'AIR)

With the conclusion of the successful British/American campaign in North Africa, agreement was reached with the French to train and re-equip their air units which had been stationed in French North African territories. In 1943 the USAAF became chiefly responsible for this task and in March 1944 began converting Hurricane-equipped units to P-47Ds. By May the *4eme Escadre de Chasse* (equivalent to an RAF wing) was established in Corsica, with two *Groupes de Chasse* (equivalent to RAF squadrons), each having an establishment of 16 P-47Ds. Later in the summer of 1944 a third *Groupe de Chasse*, was also operational in Corsica in a fighter bomber role. All units subsequently moved to southern France as part of the 1st French Air Corps, 1st Tactical Air Force. These Thunderbolt units operated in support of US and French ground forces, moving through Alsace into Germany. A second P-47-equipped *Escadre* was formed late in 1944 and went into action during the final months of the war. The French retained Thunderbolts in service squadrons until 1960. Apart from a numerical designation, every *Groupe de Chasse* was named for a French colony or province.

Groupe de Chasse	Escadre	Active – Inactive	Model
II/5 'La Fayette'	4	3/44-7/47	P-47D
II/3 'Dauphine'	4	5/44-7/47	P-47D
I/4 'Navarre'	3 & 4	7/44-7/47	P-47D
I/5 'Champagne'	3	9/44-7/47	P-47D
III/3 'Ardennes'	4	10/44-3/46	P-47D
III/6 'Roussillon'	3	2/45-3/46	P-47D

Post-War French Use

The wartime units GC II/3 and GC II/5 of *4ème Escadre* were redesignated GC I/4 and GC II/4 respectively on 1 July 1947. They continued to operate P-47Ds as part of the French occupational air forces in Germany until late 1949 and early 1950. GC I/4 and GC I/5, the wartime units forming *3ème Escadre* were also redesignated on 1 July 1947, as GC I/3 and GC II/3. Shortly afterwards the personnel of the *3ème Escadre* were sent to Indo-China where other aircraft types were flown. Returning to France late in 1948, the *Escadre* again operated P-47s, for a year until converting to jets in 1950.

Other post-war units flying P-47s were: GC I/1 'Provence' (2/50–9/51), GC II/1 'Nice' (11/50–7/51), GC I/2 'Cigognes' (1946–3/49), GC III/2 'Alsace' (1/48–49), GC I/8 'Mahgreb' (1956), GC II/8 'Languedoc' (8/51–1/52), GC I/6 'Corse' (6/49–12/49) GC II/6 'Normandie–Niémen' (12/51–4/54) and GC I/21 'Artois' (1951–52).

GC I/10, GC II/10 and GC III/10 were established from reserve training units in 1951, the first two becoming EEC† II/17 and GEC‡ III/17 in 1954, EEC I/17 was formed the same year. In 1956 these operational training units were formed into the 20ème Escadre for combat operations in Algeria. GC I/20 'Ayres–Nementcha' operated P-47s from January 1957 until mid-1958, but GC II/20 'Ouarsénis' continued to fly the type until early in 1960. GC III/20 'Oranie' (formed from GC I/6 in 1956) operated as the P-47 operational training unit of 20ème Escadre.

Additionally there were a number of small specialised units operating P-47s for various duties:- liaison, experimentation, training, etc.

Air National Guard Use

The flying element of state territorial forces, the National Guard, operated P-47s between 1946 and 1955. The original post-war plan called for ANG units located east of the Mississippi to fly P-47s and those to the west to operate P-51s. There was some divergence but this plan was broadly adhered to as can be seen from the following list of units.

101 FS	Massachusetts	F-47N
104 FS	Maryland	F-47D
105 FS	Tennessee	F-47N
118 FS	Connecticut	F-47D/N
121 FS	District of Columbia	F-47N
128 FS	Georgia	F-47D
131 FS	Massachusetts	F-47N
132 FS	Maine	F-47N
133 FS	New Hampshire	F-47D
134 FS	Vermont	F-47N
136 FS	New York	F-47D
141 FS	New Jersey	F-47N
142 FS	Delaware	F-47N
143 FS	Rhode Island	F-47D (little use)
146 FS	Pennsylvania	F-47N
149 FS	Virginia	F-47N
153 FS	Mississippi	F-47N
156 FS	North Carolina	F-47D
157 FS	South Carolina	F-47D
158 FS	Georgia	F-47D
166 FS	Ohio	F-47D (little use)
167 FS	West Virginia	F-47N
198 FS	Puerto Rico	F-47N
199 FS	Hawaii	F-47N

† *Escadron d'Entrainment à la Chasse*
‡ *Groupe d'Entrainment à la Chasse*

149

Index

150

151